Ancient Jewish and Greek Encouragement and Consolation in Sorrow and Calamity.

A LECTURE

GIVEN BEFORE THE

West London Synagogue Association

ON

SUNDAY, JULY 9TH, 1916,

AND NOW EXPANDED AND ENLARGED

BY

C. G. MONTEFIORE.

WIPF & STOCK · Eugene, Oregon

Wipf and Stock Publishers
199 W 8th Ave, Suite 3
Eugene, OR 97401

Ancient Jewish and Greek Encouragement and
 Consolation in Sorrow and Calamity
A Lecture Given Before the West London Synagogue Association on
 Sunday, July 9th, 1916 and Now Expanded and Enlarged
By Montefiore, Claude G.
ISBN 13: 978-1-62032-382-3
Publication date 7/15//2012
Previously published by Self, 1917

TO

Mrs. NATHANIEL L. COHEN.

THIS little essay owes its existence to you, for it was your suggestion that I should write out and print the lecture which I gave before the West London Synagogue Association at its annual meeting in July, 1916. After long delays and interruptions, your kind wish has, at last, been carried out. I am sorry that the result is not more worthy of your acceptance, but, nevertheless, I should like to adorn my small pamphlet by inscribing your name upon it, and by thus associating it with one whose work is both so widely known and so widely honoured.

C.G.M.

May, 1917.

Ancient Jewish and Greek Encouragement and Consolation in Sorrow and Calamity.

We all know what we mean when we speak of consolation, comfort, and encouragement. The title, therefore, of this essay needs no explanation. Yet it may be interesting to call to mind the derivation of the three substantives. As regards the second and third, that derivation is obvious. To comfort is to strengthen, to fortify. To encourage is to instil, or to restore, endurance and valour. Wherefore comfort and encouragement practically mean one and the same thing. The root meaning of consolation is less obvious. The Latin *solacium*, solace, and *solor*, I console, are apparently connected with the word *sollus*, and with the Greek word *holos*, meaning whole. Thus to solace would signify to make whole or sound, to repair, as we might put it, an injured spirit, a broken faith. Comfort, we may say (recalling the connection of courage with *cor*), is " to revive the heart " (Isaiah, LVII. 15).

So much for my title. The appositeness of the subject at the present time needs no proof.

The two great moral teachers of Europe have been the Hebrew and the Greek. It cannot then be devoid of interest to bring together and to consider—perhaps also, in some degree, to compare and to contrast—what these two ancient teachers have said and thought upon this absorbing subject.

Yet before we open the enquiry, which, be it observed, is primarily an historical enquiry—what, as a matter of fact, were the various old Greek and Hebrew consolations against adversity and sorrow—some few general remarks are requisite, or, at least, desirable. We had better, I think, make clear to ourselves the various kinds and sorts of evils and sorrows for which encouragement may be sought, and also, though with utmost brevity, how far men's general view or estimate of the world have affected their opinions or appraisements of sorrows and of evils.

We may classify sorrows, evils and calamities in more than one way. There are the calamities which come to an individual; there are the calamities which affect a group, a community, a tribe, a state. Again, there are evils which seem to belong to man as man, as, for instance, death, if death be accounted an evil: there are evils which seem exceptional and unusual. Much more important than these classifications is the now usual and well-known division of evils into moral and physical evils. We can use this division to distinguish evils which are the result of human sin from those which are not. Thus a tidal wave, spreading ruin and desolation over a large tract of country, is a purely physical evil: but a war, which causes similar ruin and desolation, is a moral evil; it is the result of human sin. Or, again, we may call physical evils those which affect the body; pain, disease, death. Moral evils will be those which affect the soul: sin itself, in all its ramifications and varieties. Again, to an individual, evils may be of three classes according as they arise: (a) independently of human fault, (b) through the individual's fault, error, or sin (intentional or unintentional), (c) through the faults, errors or sins of others. There are evils, again, which almost elude any classification, such as, idiocy, madness; the problem of savagery; the immense wastage of humanity, and so on. We can hardly allow that the appallingly slow growth of man from the animal to the savage, and from the savage to the civilised being; or (even worse) the dying away of the savage at the advent of " civilisation " (as in the case of the Australian aborigines), are in any valid sense man's fault. Yet they constitute problems, and can hardly be called other than " evils." We may, again, look at the actual evils around us in another way, and seek to group them into evils which ennoble, and evils which degrade. But this is scarcely a feasible classification, for the evils which degrade one man may ennoble another.

Ancient thought did not realise many of these distinctions and classifications, and with its more limited knowledge some of the problems of evil which press so heavily upon us (e.g., idiocy, savagery, hereditary disease) were hardly known or appreciated. Hence we must not expect to find replies in either old Greek or old Hebrew (including Rabbinic) literature to many of our modern difficulties. They are simply ignored. To these we must fashion, as best we can, our own palliatives and explanations.

Now I have repeatedly used the word " problem." But not all " evils " are necessarily problems. At least, they are only problems to those who have reached a certain stage of thought. And, again, an evil may be, or may not be, a " problem," as men fit it in, or cannot fit it in, with their general conception of the world. Or this very conception may make what is an evil to one man by no means an evil to another.

Thus, to take the last point first, if life itself appears, on the whole, to be an evil, death (whether our own death or the death of those we love) assumes a very different aspect from that which it wears to those to whom life is unhesitatingly a good. The " comfort " sought by the one would be unlike the " comfort " sought by the other. Thus Jewish " comfort " would be unlike Buddhist " comfort."

The old Greek historian Herodotus tells of a Thracian tribe whose custom was when a child was born, " that the nearest of kin sat round it and made lamentation for all the evils of which he must fulfil the measure, enumerating the whole number of human ills; but when a man died, they covered him up in the earth with sport and rejoicing, saying at the same time from what great evils he had escaped and was now in perfect bliss."[1]

If much is expected from life, failure and misfortune may be a greater puzzle than where life is looked at as a poor thing and a miserable experience, even at the best. Even to the same man certain " evils " may seem different at different periods of his own life. Thus about the " evil " of death, Sirach exclaims:

" O death, how bitter is the thought of thee to a man that is at peace in his possessions, unto the man that has nothing to worry about, and has prosperity in all things, and that still has strength to receive food. O death, how acceptable is thy sentence unto a man that is indigent, or that is failing in strength, or that is in extreme old age, or that is worried about all things, or is perverse and has lost patience."[2]

An evil may be greatly intensified by its *constituting* a " problem." Let us, for instance, be wholly convinced in our minds that no supernatural or divine order exists. Let us be convinced that there exists nothing but mechanical law or chance—and that what we call " morality " is the purely human creation of an hour, limited to a transitory earth. In one way, indeed, evil may seem worse. For there is clearly in it no purpose; and there is no escape from it except by our unaided wills. But, in another way, it is less burdensome, for it is no longer a puzzle. There is no agonised cry, " How can the good God allow or create this evil?", for we no longer believe in any good God. Job could not, it is true, have been consoled by the divine theophany. But, on the other hand, his pain would have been less poignant. For his pain was mental. The main agony was not the keen physical suffering, or the mere *fact* of his losses, but it was largely the *interpretation* of the suffering and the losses, or rather that he could not fit them in with his old belief in a righteous and omnipotent God. The supposed injustice of his woes was the sharpest sting in them.

Comfort is required not merely for calamity as such, but for calamity in relation to desert, in relation to a supposed moral interpretation of the world as a whole, and as governed by supernatural, divine beings. Anxiety as to the moral meaning or bearing of calamity adds to its severity. We have examples of this every day. You slip upon the carpet, and break your arm. You may need encouragement to bear the pain, but it constitutes no puzzle to you, and neither worries you nor your friends. But if, in the fulness of a man's powers and usefulness, he is struck down by a long and painful disease, we ask at once: "What is the meaning of such a misfortune? How can it be fitted in with our faith in the providential order of the world?" The naked facts of evil and calamity upon the assumption of an entirely godless world would carry with them no added sting. There would be no divine " comfort "; but there would be no spiritual conflict. And we may say that the more powerful, the more unique, the more loving, the God in whom a man believes, the sharper and greater can become the problem, though we may also add the nobler and purer and more satisfying can become the consolation and the comfort.

If the God is regarded as omnipotent, and if there is supposed to be no other divine power than He, then for all evil and calamity He is ultimately responsible. At this stage the problem attains its height, and the tension—between the supposed righteousness of God, on the one hand, and the facts of evil, upon the other—is stretched to the utmost. But various stages of development may be gone through before this sharpest tension is reached. And when it is reached, the solution may be sought in a variety of ways.

Early Jewish thought upon the whole subject was very simple. Reflection had not gone far; the gravity of the problem was not yet felt or recognised. And as men could not yet possess or appreciate the highest and purest consolations, so they also had not to wrestle with too grievous a problem, or to support too heavy a burden. The wind was tempered to the lamb.

So far as we can make out, as we seek to pierce the mist in which the thoughts of those far off times lie covered, individuals took themselves less seriously than we do. Troubles which befell them or their friends caused them less mental anguish than they cause us. They worried far less about their meaning. They did not seek to relate them to the Divine goodness or justice. God busied himself, and was concerned, less with the individual than with Israel as a whole.

Moreover, so far as any particular calamity was brought into sharp relation with God at all—and naturally the bigger, the stranger, the more unusual the calamity, the more natural it was, and the more urgent it seemed, to do this,—it was not yet supposed that God must have some essentially *moral* purpose in bringing the calamity about. His ways were unaccountable: men had to accept them: it was not sought, for it was not possible, to explain them.

Next, the distinction between moral and physical evil had not yet arisen before the mind. As a clear and theoretic distinction we may indeed say that the Hebrews and the Jews never attained to it at all. It was the creation of the Greek philosophers.

Yet very early in Hebrew thought a fundamental ethical idea about suffering took hold of the people: it was the idea that suffering and evil and calamity are retribution and punishment for committed sin. This idea, which, in a more spiritual form, and with many modifications and qualifications, Judaism still retains, was of immense importance. It was a support and a comfort: it was also to prove in later days a puzzle and a problem.

In the earlier period the retribution and punishment conception of suffering and calamity was much more acceptable and less difficult than it afterwards became, because of two other ideas that accompanied it. The first of these was the idea of human, or rather of national, solidarity. That idea was the reflection of facts with which we are all familiar, facts which are as true now as they were true then, though the interpretation which we give to them is different. For in our time, too, the sin of one may involve the misery of many, and a family or a state, by the guilt of its chief, may become involved in a common calamity. To the Israelite of old this fact hardly involved a problem. The unit of personality was rather the whole than its parts. The family or the nation was the moral agent even more than the individuals who composed it. It was not unjust that all should suffer through the guilt of one; the parts could not grumble if they had to share in a common lot. It was obvious, for instance, that the results of the King's deeds, including their punishments, must affect all his subjects.

And, secondly, if the unit of personality was the whole, of which many individuals formed the parts, this whole was, in a sense, immortal, or at least continuous. A family or a nation lives on: its parts die, and are born anew. Thus it is not unjust, but it is obvious and fitting, that the good or the evil which is wrought by the parts should affect one generation after another. And the retribution (or the reward) which follows those deeds of good and evil may affect a second or a third generation as reasonably and obviously as it may affect contemporaries.

Thus when God was more and more supposed to be the dispenser of good and evil, and the just bestower of reward and retribution, He too must act upon these obvious and reasonable lines. He must visit the iniquity of the fathers upon the sons and the grandsons. The family or the nation is the unit of personality. Whether the retribution (or the reward) hits one generation or another, one link or a second, makes no difference. It is the same unit, the same whole, which has been hit. It is, indeed, a solemn declaration of the free, powerful and compassionate agency of God when it is stated that He visits for punishment only unto the third and fourth generation, but far more widely and generously for compassion and for good.[3] Thus the amplification of the Second Commandment, which was to cause much religious distress later on (and which to many simple souls still causes distress to-day), was in its own time, and when it was first formulated (the date is uncertain), an indication of religious progress. It may also be noted that this was in no wise to put the consequence of the deed into the deed itself. So far as that more inward (and more Indian) doctrine was to come at all, it was to come much later. Israelite thought tended to make the result of the deed lie less and less in the deed itself, and more and more in the outside agency of a sovereign and unaccountable (if also a righteous and a compassionate) God.

We saw that different views of life obviously change the character of the comfort which may be sought for against life's vicissitudes. The old Israelite (and the average Rabbinic Jew, who, in this respect, did not fundamentally change), had no hesitation about life. No metaphysical problems as to reality bothered him, or obscured the happiness of the sunlight. He never dreamed but that life was a good, and its cessation an evil. He never considered it an illusion. He never supposed that there was some deeper and truer life beyond its masks and shows, to which thinking, on the one hand, or purity of soul, upon the other, could make a man attain. The only other life was a life far poorer than this life: it was the shadowy, empty, and vapid life of Sheol, that wretched and feeble life after death to which all men must, alas, come, and from which no man could be delivered. In this regard the old Israelite was at one with

Homer and Achilles. Nor had the old Israelite any contempt of or disapproval for the material things of life, for flocks and herds and fig trees and vines, for silver and gold. These things were good, and the lack of them was evil. And though a higher insight and a better appraisement were to come, Judaism has never denied the " goodness " of material things. Wisdom is far better than rubies, but rubies are not wholly to be despised. Not a contempt for the material, but the right use of it; not the hatred of the body, but its cleanly sanctification, became the doctrine of Judaism.

We know and hear little how, in early days, the Israelite sought comfort in sorrow and consolation in calamity. Simple resignation, not yet of a deeply ethical kind, appears to be the attitude of early piety. Thus when Eli hears from Samuel of the trouble which is in store for him, he replies with simple dignity : "It is Yahweh; let Him do what seems good to Him."[4] But this utterance, manly as it is, is yet very far from the ethical depth of the famous aphorism of Job. Yahweh is still not wholly moralised : you have just to take what comes from Him, and bear it as best you may. The stage of complaint is higher than this earlier stage of resignation, because complaint means that the calamity complained of is hard to reconcile with the assumed goodness of God. " Righteous art thou, O Lord, *therefore* will I plead with thee."[5] Till there is an ampler belief in the righteousness, the pleadings cannot arise. Nevertheless, this less ethical resignation does not preclude high courage in the hour of danger : as Joab said to Abishai, his brother, before the battle, " Be of good courage, and let us play the men for our people and for the cities of our God, and let Yahweh do that which seems good to Him."[6]

In the early days of ethical monotheism—even to so rigid a moralist as Amos, the earliest of the great prophets, and in some ways the purest of his type—the difficulty involved in the good and just God being the cause of apparent evil had not arisen. To Amos, God is the cause of all things—both good and evil, and he seems to find no difficulty in such a conception. He is not at pains with some modern teachers (in the pious innocence of their hearts) to declare that the evil, because it comes from the " just " God, must be only " apparent," or disciplinal, or the inevitable, if painful, harbinger of good. Quite simply and naively, and in happy unconsciousness of the problem, he cries out: " Shall a trumpet be blown in the city, and the people not be afraid? Shall there be evil in a city, and

Yahweh not have done it?" (Whether we translate the Hebrew word by " evil " or by " calamity " makes no difference here).'

It is only when the problem begins to be felt that the consolation became more interesting. For the two things go together. Till the sting is realised, the salve cannot be applied. The problem starts with the relation of suffering to desert. Why do the righteous suffer? Why are the wicked prosperous? For this is the simplest of the problems, and the most fundamental. Once felt, it can never be wholly ignored. Other and deeper problems may appear upon the horizon, but this old and simple one never loses its interest and its poignancy. It became acute in Israel because of the extraordinary, and often unwholesome and unsatisfactory, development of the doctrine of retribution. God rewards the righteous; He punishes the wicked. The very existence of religion; the very *raison d'être* for the worship of God, seemed inextricably mixed up with these assertions. They were felt as regards the individual; they were felt as regards the nation. And as the individual became more and more of a separate personality, demanding his own relation to, and his own just and separate treatment from, God, the problem became of necessity more acute. As reflection grew, the mournful lot of man was more fully realised. What comforts could be discovered for these sorrows and perplexities? Till the belief in a future life of blessedness and felicity arose, the comforts tended to become inadequate in relation to the sorrows. The perplexities outgrew and outweighed the explanations.

The book of Job gives classic expression to the heightened sense of sadness concerning man and his lot. It may indeed be said that the pessimistic tone of the famous fourteenth chapter goes beyond the average Israelite and Jewish level. It accentuates the sad side of life more than is usual.

" Man that is born of woman is of few days and full of trouble. He comes forth like a flower, and withers: he flees as a shadow, and does not abide." And again: " Is there not a hard service for man upon earth? Are not his days like the days of a hireling?"

Genius and the awakening sense of individuality put the difficulty involved in the divine visitation of the sins of the fathers upon the children with unexampled force and bitterness.

" God layeth up—do ye say?—his iniquity for his children? Nay: let Him requite it to *himself* that *he* may feel it! Let his own eyes see his destruction, and let him drink of the wrath of the Almighty! For what concern has he in his house after him, when the number of his months is fulfilled?"

And then the simple problem of the relation of prosperity and adversity to conduct and desert is summed up in words of wonderful simplicity and pathos.

"One dies in his full strength, being wholly at ease and quiet. His pails are full of milk, and the marrow of his bones is moistened. And another dies in the bitterness of his soul, and has never tasted happiness. They lie down alike in the dust and the worms cover them."[8] The author of Ecclesiastes, with his "one event to all," could not put his complaint with greater vividness than this.

Occasionally, but very rarely, in the Hebrew Scriptures a deeper note is heard. If God is omnipotent, why did He make man so feeble and so frail? Even suppose that all calamity and suffering are the results of sin, even suppose that the righteous few must suffer with the guilty many (suffer *with*, not suffer *for*, except in the theology of the Babylonian Isaiah), or even suppose that the son must suffer for the wickedness of his parents, why was man *allowed* to sin at all? Wherefore this heart so sick and so deceitful? But this deeper and more searching question is hardly yet raised. For reasons of His own God may even specially cause, and stimulate, a man to sin. God hardens Pharoah's heart. For an unexplained reason He is angry with Israel, and therefore incites David to commit the sin of a census. A later age *did* find this divine incitement a problem, and thought to better matters by making the entice-ment proceed not from God, but from a direct power of evil—from Satan. Isaiah could picture God as giving the order, "make the heart of this people fat, make their ears heavy, shut their eyes, so that they see not, and hear not, and understand not, and repent not, and be not healed." At the period of the exile it seemed to some as if sin had become a sort of contagion or malady from which the people could not shake themselves free. This could be even represented as an added punishment. "They shall pine away in their iniquities and in the iniquities of their fathers." Or this "pining away" could be represented as a sorrowful complaint. "Verily our sins and iniquities lie heavy upon us; we pine away in them." This uneasy feeling of compulsion, of a weight of sin which is irresistible and that cannot be thrown off, is still more clearly expressed in the ques-tion (unique, I think, in the Hebrew scriptures), "Why dost thou make us to err from thy ways; why dost thou harden our hearts from thy fear?"[9]

So far we have only heard of the presentation of problems. It is time to come to the suggested answers: to the complaints to add the consolations. Of these the most primary and the strongest is undoubtedly rooted fast in the idea of recompense. For the sorrows and afflictions of the present the future will bring a glorious requital. Israel's enemies will be punished; Israel will be happy and prosperous. In the major portion of the Hebrew Bible both complaints and consolations have a national reference. Even in the Psalter it is probable that almost every Psalm in its existing form has a more or less distinct and direct reference to the community, or to a section or group within the community. The afflictions of which the writers complain are probably not purely individual afflictions, but afflictions which have befallen them in virtue of their being members of the group or of the community as a whole. And the recompense which is demanded, prayed for, believed in, is not primarily a recompense of satisfaction. It is a religious recompense, needed for the justification of God. " A neutral God is no God. God does not exist for men, if He makes no difference between those who seek Him and those who pay no heed to Him. Then is piety an illusion ; it stretches its hands into the empty air, and meets no divine Arm for it to grasp. Piety needs reward, not for the sake of the reward, but to be assured of its own reality, to know that there is for a surety a communion with God and an access to His grace."[10] The most genuine and most original Israelite and Jewish consolation is thus the Messianic hope. Israel, justified by suffering and punishment, shall once more be " happy and glorious." Inward and outward well being, moral righteousness and material prosperity, shall be its lot. There can be no doubt that this belief, from the time when it was first accepted by the nation, on the strength of prophetic utterances often repeated, right on throughout the ages, has been a " comfort " of enormous potency. And it has been an altruistic comfort. That is to say, even though the sufferer did not suppose that he would himself witness and experience the glory and the felicity, yet his faith was strengthened and his heart was satisfied by the conviction that a future generation would assuredly enjoy them. It is not wonderful that when the great deliverance was supposed to be near at hand—and the interval between Announcement and Fulfilment was constantly foreshortened by faith—the expectation of it was an immense consolation. It is much more striking that the hope was a potent balsam, even when its realization was thought to be in a less immediate future. It could constitute such a comfort even without any belief in a future life of happiness for the sufferer himself, partly by means of a pure and noble patriotism or, again, of a pure and noble, if half conscious, feeling, " So long as God really cares for Israel and Righteousness, never mind what happens to me," but partly too by the conception, then and for long accepted without much cavil, that a people or a state formed a unity—almost a single moral personality—throughout the ages. It could be so all the more, so long, and so far, as the transient individual identified himself with the permanent nation; the mortal Israelite with the immortal Israel. Under such conditions it was enough for the sufferer to look forward to, and to believe in, a time of outward and inward happiness— of material prosperity and of extended or even universal right-eousness—in which he himself should have no share. Later on such an altruism was hardly possible. An awakened individual-ism demanded more personal attention. A distant Messianic age could not roll away the stumbling block before the pure justice of God. Promised felicity to-morrow does not remove the sting of no felicity to-day, when to-morrow's felicity is not to be tasted by to-day's sufferer; nor does even the righteousness of the future entirely compensate for, and explain, the iniquity of the present. Hence it was that the Messianic hope had to be supplemented by a hope more personal and universal—the hope of resurrection and immortality. We can see how, in one of the latest predictions of the Hebrew Bible, the second hope is coming into birth to strengthen and supplement the first. We can, perhaps, hardly disentangle the two hopes in those famous words of comfort: " He will annihilate death for ever, and the Lord God will wipe away tears from off all faces," of which Dr. Skinner truly says, " Perhaps no words that ever were uttered have sunk deeper into the aching heart of humanity than this exquisite image of the Divine tenderness."[11]

It would, however, be needless, or take too long, to bring together the progress of Messianic consolation in the Prophetical literature. It is not certain how often the anticipated or pre-dicted joys and deliverances in the Psalter are to be interpreted in a specially Messianic sense. Very often they doubtless only allude to a nearer and more limited future, which is to wipe away the memory of a painful present. The faith of the Psalmists—their acceptance of the Prophetic teachings—made them grandly optimistic. The gloom, the persecution, the sorrow, would surely pass: God would soon vindicate those who trusted in His goodness. "Weeping may tarry for a night, but joy cometh in the morning." So far as the individual was concerned an immense stress was laid upon the end. It was not, as Wellhausen says, that these pious souls yearned for an equivalent amount of prosperity to compensate them for a great amount of suffering. What they wanted was a proof to themselves and to others of the righteousness of their cause and of themselves, a proof of God's concern and solicitude, a proof of His interest and His power. This was the more urgently necessary because only in this earthly life could that vindication take place. Even a short duration of happiness and peace before the end would be sufficient for this all-important purpose. A final deliverance would show that the Lord does in truth, as faith declared, deliver the righteous out of his afflictions. Hence the eagerness and anxiety of so many of the prayers: make haste to save before it shall be too late; tarry not in rescue and justification.

Yet the highest teaching of the Psalter and its deepest preciousness do not lie in its hopes for future deliverance, future prosperity, future vindication. In any case I will not deal further with them here, or make quotations from such familiar utterances. Let us rather turn now from hopes for the future to consolations which deal more directly with the present, and which may be felt by the individual sufferer, even apart from the future of his community or from his own.

Shall we recall, first of all, that consolation or palliative, common both to Greek and Hebrew, and almost sure to suggest itself at a certain stage of reflection to the human mind and heart? Suffering is a discipline; a purification. The proud are humbled by it; the ignorant are taught by it; the careless are reminded by it of God and the eternal verities. This view, or explanation, of suffering, however inadequate, has yet served to many as a comfort and an encouragement. The Old Testament thinkers several times allude to the chastening or correction which is rather disciplinal than retributive. Thus we all remember the famous verse in Deuteronomy: "As a man chastens his son, so the Lord thy God chastened thee." The hunger of the desert was a deliberate proving and humiliation. The words of Deuteronomy are echoed by the Psalmist and the Sage. And no teaching became more repeated and familiar: "It is good for me that I have been afflicted that I might learn thy statutes." "Despise not the chastening of the Lord; be not weary of His correction. For whom the Lord loves He corrects; He gives pain to the son in whom He delights."[12]

It is needless to do more than just allude to the many parallel passages. There is the Psalmist's exclamation: "Happy is the man whom thou chastenest, O Lord"; there is the warning of Eliphaz: "Happy is the man whom God corrects: despise not thou the chastening of the Almighty. For He makes sore and binds up, He wounds and His hands make whole." Less known, but even more striking, are words that occur at the opening of a very difficult and very corrupt passage in the third speech of Elihu. The words apparently hit the keynote of Elihu's argument. Sorrow purifies: it prevents the germination of a false self-confidence and an illegitimate pride. "He delivers the afflicted through his affliction; He opens his ear through suffering."[13]

By the prophets, too, the idea of the purification of sorrow is made use of. "I will refine them as silver is refined; I will try them as gold is tried." It is curious that the famous phrase in Isaiah, "I have tried thee in the furnace of affliction," may rest upon a correction of the original text. A psalmist repeats the metaphor, together with others. "Thou hast tried us as silver is tried; thou broughtest us into the net, thou laidst a heavy burden upon our loins; thou didst cause men to ride over our heads; we went through fire and through water; but thou broughtest us out into freedom."[14]

That there may be a meaning in suffering—a value in it, a glorification of it, an explanation of it—by its being looked at as undergone consciously and willingly for a cause or for a person, is very rarely alluded to in the Hebrew Scriptures. Suffering as service, as devotion to a cause or a person, is very seldom referred to. This particular explanation and palliative was, it would seem, little known in Biblical times. We may note the cry in the Maccabean psalm: "For thy sake are we killed all the day long: we are counted as sheep for the slaughter." But the cry is a complaint. There is no indication (as in the dying words of Akiba) that the cause transfigured the suffering, and made it glorious. This note is struck in the words of Judas before his last battle: words fitly chosen as the motto for the beautiful monument to Admiral Craddock in York Minster. The Authorised Version's rendering of the Greek (itself a translation of a lost Hebrew original) is loose, but in the spirit true: "If our time be come, let us die manfully for our brethren's sake, and let us not stain our honour."[15] There is indeed one sublime passage in which the doctrine of the conscious acceptance of suffering, the deliberate shouldering of pain, for the sake of others is definitely taught. It is hardly necessary to say that I am thinking of the great fifty-third chapter of Isaiah. Here those who have been converted to righteousness and the knowledge of God by the sufferings of the Servant realise that these very sufferings were deliberately undergone for the sake of the end, for the sake of others. It was therefore that the Servant gave his back to the smiters and his cheeks to them that plucked out the hair; that he hid not his face from shame and spitting. It was therefore that he let himself be afflicted and oppressed, that he was brought as a lamb to the slaughter, and opened not his mouth. It was done in faithfulness; it was done in unselfishness; it was done deliberately; in order that through this suffering and affliction, through this patient martyrdom and death, peace and healing and the turning away from iniquity might come to many. Even in the midst of his sufferings he made intercession for the transgressors who smote him.

This sublime conception was for a long while not used again. And perhaps it is true to say that a totally inadequate use has been made of it, because of its central importance in the theology of a rival faith. It is indeed a great misfortune that Judaism should so greatly have ignored (and even sometimes sought to misinterpret and to cheapen) one of the noblest of its own spiritual creations.

But I have still not mentioned the great central and fundamental comfort which Biblical Judaism achieved or discovered. This comfort is most significantly and impressively expressed and illustrated in the Psalter. It may be said to consist in the very fact of God's existence, of His character, of His relation to the believer, and of the believer's relation to Him. God is good and near : He does not afflict willingly or grieve the children of men. And man can feel, can experience, this nearness of God. Hence in the very midst of trouble—illuminating and alleviating it—this consciousness of God's presence comforts and consoles. It is not, by any means, merely a belief that requital or recompense will come in the end, whether to the sufferer or to his community. It involves such a belief, but is by no means identical with it. It is far more intimate, spiritual, immediate. Quite apart from the future, and without a reckoning upon its advent, God is a comfort *now*. The Authorized Version's rendering of Psalm XLVI. 1. (based upon the Great Bible of 1539 and due to Coverdale) is inaccurate, but exceedingly illuminating; it gives the spirit of a hundred passages : " God is our refuge and strength: a *very present* help in trouble." That, then, is the great consolation. In one way or another, God is a very present help in trouble and affliction. Here, again, after noting and emphasizing the fact, it is unnecessary to illustrate it by quotations: they are too obvious and familiar. The variations upon the theme are endless. God is a shield and a buckler; He is a rock and a stronghold; He is a light in darkness; under the shadow of His wings men take refuge. In Him the believer finds rest and calm and confidence and hope. Nearness to Him is a joy and delight. This great fact of God's existence, this experienced communion with Him, this realisation of His nearness, this conviction of His fidelity and His goodness, are themselves a consolation in the very midst of suffering, and while the issue of it is still uncertain and future. ' He heals the broken hearted and binds up their wounds ': He does this not merely in the future—that is to say, the idea is not merely that adversity shall be succeeded by prosperity—but He does it in the very midst of sorrow. He Himself and the thought of Him are a *present* consolation. Thus we find a Psalmist saying: ' In the multitude of my cares within me, Thy comforts delight my soul.'

To the man who can say, " There is naught upon earth that I desire beside thee," it is not unreasonable that, though his physical power is failing, God should remain the " strength of his heart and his portion for ever." It is also noticeable—and as a transition to Rabbinic Judaism very important—how to the author of the 119th psalm the comforts of God are as it were embodied in the Law. " This is my comfort in my affliction: thy word has kept me alive." " Unless," he says, and he speaks for all pious Israelites, " unless thy law had been my delight, I should have perished in my affliction." " Trouble and anguish have taken hold of me; yet thy commandments are my delight." In other words outward and physical suffering cannot take away, but on the contrary, quicken the apprehension of, the comforts and the joys of religion. God is realised in the very midst of sorrow. It was a wonderful discovery; a permanent triumph of the soul.[16]

To the problem of sin and of the evil heart, mentioned by certain prophets as already troubling the mind, the Biblical writers hardly give any other answer than the possibility of repentance. That possibility is very rarely denied. To it Ezekiel more especially adds the promise of a new heart from God. The two conceptions are placed side by side: no attempt is made to harmonize them. " Repent and make you a new heart," (it is assumed that "where there is a will there is a way," and "that it is never too late to mend.") And then again, "A new heart and a new spirit will I give you; I will remove the stony heart, and I will give you a heart of flesh." In other words the burden of sin may be broken by man's will and by the grace of God. The conquest is both "natural" and "supernatural" in one.[17]

For the rest, Old Testament piety trusts with touching fidelity in the righteousness and wisdom of God. This trust reaches its highest point in the two famous utterances of Job, and it is interesting and curious that the book, from which we can draw the most bitter denunciations of the world order and the rule of God, contains also the two most familiar and comprehensive statements of unquestioning resignation and faith. "The Lord gave, the Lord has taken away; blessed be the name of the Lord." "Shall we receive good at the hand of God, and shall we not receive evil?" In the second utterance we may note that no difficulty or hesitation is felt in ascribing "evil" (or "calamity") to the direct agency of the Divine Being.

The limitation of almost the whole Old Testament outlook to an earthly future—the absence of any belief in a resurrection of the body or in the immortality of the "soul"—put faith in divine justice to a severe trial. Yet, as we have seen, in spite of the growing claims of the individual, piety on the whole stood the test nobly. When the strain became too intense, the belief in a blessed future beyond the grave providentially appeared. On the one hand, the Old Testament period may be said to end for a small minority in the sadness and semi-pessimism of Ecclesiastes ("One lot to the good and to the bad; vanity of vanities"); on the other hand, for the large majority, faith in the divine goodness is still retained. It is retained partly by a passionate conviction that for the community, at any rate, the future will surely bring both inward and outward well-being and felicity, and partly by a trust in God and a life with God, which even the inevitable advent of death is powerless to shake or to destroy. Between the two extremes of sad scepticism and triumphant faith, intermediate tones of despondency, struggling with the search for God, can also be heard. An example of such a struggle is the 39th psalm, and the different views of the commentators are instructive. The difficulty is to gauge with accuracy the exact spiritual implications of many Old Testament passages, and not least of many a Psalm. The vexed question of the "I" of the Psalter (is an individual speaking or the community?) constantly makes itself felt. There is also a certain uncertainty of touch, a certain vacillation, in the 39th Psalm, which partly accounts for the different judgments of the commentators. Thus there is doubtless some justification for Wellhausen: "The Psalmist's resignation borders upon depair. It is remarkable how little he desires from God. The present is cheerless; of a future world there is no thought. Faith longs for sight, but longs in vain; yet it persists, though it is almost extinguished by the painful contradiction which experience brings." Shall we rather say that, in spite of the Psalmist's sadness, he has not lost his faith in the divine righteousness? If so, there is justification for those noble words of Delitzsch, which this very Psalm suggests to him. "That is just the heroic feature in the faith of the Old Testament, that, in the midst of the riddles of this life, and face to face with the impenetrable darkness resting on the life beyond, it throws itself without reserve into the arms of God." Yet the dawn of "the larger hope" did not break before it was sorely needed.

The close of the Old Testament period—i.e., the middle of the second century B.C.—witnessed its coming. In one famous passage, the date of which is practically known (166 B.C.), we find the doctrine of the resurrection of the righteous and of the wicked clearly enunciated. "Many of them that sleep in the dust of the earth shall awake, some to everlasting life, and some to shame and everlasting abhorrence."[18] The language is quite plain: the meaning is evident. Before another century was over, the doctrine had become general and common. At the beginning of the first century A.D. the Pharisees teach it; the Sadducees reject it. In the Rabbinic literature it is as much a dogma of the faith as the existence of God.

Looking at the doctrine as a consolation, we might at first sight be disposed to think that, in some respects, it is less pure a comfort than the old faith which "threw itself without reserve into the arms of God." And, perhaps, for a chosen soul here and there, that may be the case. We remember the mediæval story of the woman who desired to destroy the hope of heaven and the fear of hell, so that men might love God without anticipation of punishment or of reward. But religion is for the many, and not only for the few. The future life was needed as a stimulus and a comfort. It is needed even now, and men still believe in it. Yet our view of it has considerably changed, and to us it is a stimulus and a comfort for not quite the same reasons as to our ancestors.

It may be, and it is, a consolation to us to believe that those we love who have been sorely tried on earth shall know peace and happiness beyond the grave, but we have got beyond the stage of finding any consolation in believing that the wicked shall be punished in " hell." The truth is that we want the future life less for the good than for the bad : and we want it for them less as a punishment than as a purification. But our ancestors needed it in order to be able to believe in the *justice* of God; and this justice seemed to them to involve proportionate (or rather—and most unhappily—disproportionate) requital. Temporary sorrows of the " good " seemed to require endless " reward "; temporary wickedness (or prosperity) of the bad seemed to require endless " punishment." It was very untoward and unfortunate that death usually seemed to shut the door upon advance or development. The life of the resurrection, the life of the world to come, the life of Eden, or the life of Gehenna, would not be a world of gradual improvement for the " good " and of gradual purification for the " wicked." The more usual idea was that " heaven " and " hell " were alike fixed. Static beatitude in the one ; static discomfort in the other : earth alone the period of development.

Gigantically important, then, from every point of view as the doctrine of a future life was in the history of Judaism, great as the support of the belief was to every generation of the faithful, it is yet the least interesting of all those Rabbinic comforts and consolations which go beyond the comforts and the consolations of the Hebrew Bible. But its power was enormous. The life of the Israelite was lived in close contact with the life of Israel as a whole. And this life of Israel was mainly a life of sorrow and misfortune. Nevertheless, great though the sins of Israel might be in relation to an ideal standard, or in relation to the demands of the Law, Israel in relation to the gentile or Christian world which persecuted and oppressed, was righteous. The sinners were its enemies. Hence the doctrine, so clearly enunciated in the Talmud, which must have brought immense comfort (how can we, who live in freedom, wonder ?) to many an unfortunate household in many an age. " God brings chastisements upon the righteous in this world, that they may inherit the world to come ; He heaps prosperity upon the wicked in this world to drive them down in the next world to the lowest depth (of Gehenna)."[19] Such ideas have for us to-day little interest or

value. Yet the Rabbis were not without the doctrine—however
partially and imperfectly worked out—that the "punishments"
of the future life were not retributive but disciplinal. The
familiar *locus classicus* upon the subject runs thus: "The school
of Shammai said: There are three divisions in the day of
judgment, the completely righteous, the completely wicked, and
the inbetween. The completely righteous are inscribed and
sealed at once for Eternal Life ; the completely wicked are inscribed and sealed at once for Gehenna ; the inbetween go down
into Gehenna, and howl and come up again. But the school of
Hillel said: They who sin in the flesh among the Israelites and
among the nations go down to Gehenna, and are judged there
twelve months, and then their bodies are destroyed, and their
souls are burnt, and the wind scatters them under the soles of the
righteous. But the heretics and the informers and the apostates
and the atheists and they who deny (the divinity of) the Torah
and the resurrection of the dead, who separate themselves from
the community, who spread terror in the land, and who (not only)
sin themselves, but cause others to sin—they go down into
Gehenna, and are punished there for ever."[20]

All these speculations have lost their value for us ; yet we
may seek to judge them tenderly, and we had better draw a veil
over their childishness. We have happily risen beyond them ;
we can pass on.

More dignified and simple is the famous utterance of that
Alexandrian sage, who was, perhaps, one of the first Jews to
teach the Platonic doctrine of the immortality of the soul : "The
souls of the righteous are in the hand of God, and no torment
shall touch them. In the eyes of the foolish they seem to have
died, and their departure is accounted to be their hurt, and their
journeying away from us to be their ruin : but they are in peace.
For though in the sight of men they are punished, their own
hope is full of immortality. Having borne a little chastening,
they shall receive great good; because God has made trial of
them, and found them worthy of Himself."[21] The comfort of
these words can endure from age to age.

What the hope of resurrection meant to an era of persecution
we may gather from the story of the martyrdom of the seven sons
and their mother in the second book of Maccabees. Note the
phrases : " Thou, miscreant, dost release us out of this present
life, but the King of the world shall raise up us who have died
for His laws, unto an eternal renewal of life." And again. " It
is good to die at the hands of men, and look for the hopes which

are given by God that we shall be raised up again by Him; for as
for thee, thou shalt have no resurrection unto life." Or the
words of the mother : " Fear not this butcher, but, proving thyself worthy of thy brothers, accept thy death, that in the mercy
of God I may receive thee again with thy brothers."[22]

Perhaps the best description or the best appraisal of the life
beyond the grave which Rabbinic literature affords, are
those adages of R. Jacob which I have quoted so frequently that
I am half ashamed to quote them yet again. Yet well do they
bear a constant repetition. " This world is like a vestibule before
the world to come; prepare thyself in the vestibule that thou
mayest enter into the hall. Better is one hour of repentance
and good deeds in this world than the whole life of the world to
come ; but better is one hour of blissfulness of spirit in the world
to come than the whole life of this world."[23]

The " consolation " of the future life puts Rabbinic comforts
altogether on to a new and higher plane. So far as mere suffering is concerned (apart from the question of sin) the conviction
of a future life of blessedness fully satisfies the average believer.
The tortured soul is put to rest. With this belief a man need
neither distort facts nor question the divine justice. There was
no necessity to assume that earthly calamity was the result of
sin committed by its sufferers. It is true that Jewish thought
shook off this false idea with very great difficulty. The old view
was maintained in the well known saying of R. Ammi, " There
is no death without sin; there is no suffering without guilt." But
after an unsatisfactory discussion, the conclusion is declared to be,
There *is* a death which is not caused by sin; there *is* a suffering
which is not caused by guilt.[24] Yet the perverse errors of Job's
friends are constantly repeated—often with wilful and silly parti-
cularity—by the Rabbis. An example of this perversity, which
the doctrine of the future life makes all the more inexcusable, is
still allowed to deform and disfigure the orthodox prayer book.[25]
In no other point is our Berkeley Street prayer book more
superior to the authorized liturgy than by its omission of this
(to us) blasphemous stupidity.

By the conception of the future life it was easily possible to
soften the problem of the suffering of the righteous. For these
sufferings could be regarded as a test and trial of a man's
strength, of his fidelity; or again as a measure of his resignation
and piety; or as a means for the development of character, for
the *increase* of righteousness, or as a purification (for even the
righteous is not *perfect*). Or again if there is a future life, the

suffering of one man may not unjustly be sent to him for the benefit of another.

Thus it was that various Biblical interpretations of, and con-solations for, suffering could be (and were) deepened and expanded by the Rabbinical writers.

"Happy is the man whom thou chastenest." To the Bibli-cal writers this chastening could only be a passing or temporary experience : if more, it began to be not a happiness, but a puzzle. That is why such immense stress is laid upon a happy end, a prosperous close, to earthly life. For there was no good and blessed life to succeed it. To the Rabbis the puzzle no longer existed. Suffering could continue till death. With their too frequent tendency to suppose that all suffering must be a chas-tisement for some real or incipient sin, and with the odd, and to us moderns, curious, stress which they laid on physical pain, it is not wonderful that the Rabbis, in accordance with a doctrine we have already noticed, found easy consolation for bodily mis-fortune by the help of their firm faith in the future life. Characteristic for the Rabbinic point of view is the story about R. Eliezer and R. Akiba. The former was ill, and his disciples visited him. "They all wept except Akiba. He laughed. They said, Why do you laugh? He said, Why do you weep? They said, How shall we not weep when the Book of the Law (i.e., the learned Master) is in pain? Akiba said, That is why I laugh. So long as I saw that the Master's wine did not become sour, or his oil rancid, or his honey corrupt, or his flax ruined, I thought, Perhaps (though God forbid) the Master has already received his world (i.e., his reward), but now that I see the Master in pain, I rejoice. Then said Eliezer, Have I been wanting in any ordin-ance of the Law? Akiba replied, You have yourself taught me, There is no righteous man upon earth who does (nothing but) good and (never) sins."[26] "There is no man," said R. Alexander, "who does not experience sufferings. Happy is he who undergoes them for the sake of the Law."[27]

Sufferings, especially bodily sufferings, lead to repentance and atone for sin. Hence the Rabbis called them "beloved." Thus Hezekiah, in spite of all his trouble and toil, could not make his son Manasseh good. Nothing could do that except sufferings. For when bound with fetters and chains, he repented and confessed his sin, and was heard on high.[28]

If a man dies without having endured "sufferings," says a Rabbi, an imminent judgment awaits him. He who is forty days without sufferings has forfeited his world to come![29] Or, at any rate, a severe punishment is in store for him. As oil is obtained by beating the olive, so Israel turns to goodness only through sufferings.[30] R. Eliezer said, The blood of a wound atones like the blood of an offering. Raba qualified this statement by the observation that such atonement only operated if the blood came from the thumb of the right hand, and if the wound befell a man on his way to perform some precept of the Law.[31] It is difficult to say how far these seemingly childish remarks are to be taken seriously.

Quaint is the story of R. Chama who saw a blind man and said, Peace to thee, O freeman! How did the Rabbi know that the blind man was the son of a slave? He meant that he was a freeman of the world to come. For if the law emancipates him who suffers only in one of his limbs (Exodus XXI. 27), how much more shall *he* be emancipated (i.e., receive the world to come) who suffers in all his body.[32]

Isaac, the patriarch, wished for sufferings. He said to God, If a man die without sufferings, a severe judgment awaits him, but by sufferings (upon earth) the (future) judgment is diminished. " Thou hast desired a good thing," said God, "and I will make a beginning of sufferings with thee!" For this is the first mention of sufferings in the Torah, " And Isaac was old and he could not see."[33] The very covenant of God with Israel was only made through sufferings. The glory of the Holy One rests upon him on whom sufferings have come. Beloved are sufferings, for three good gifts were granted to Israel only through sufferings: the Law; the promised land; and the future life. That each gift was won by suffering is proved by the usual playful exegesis. Thus that the future life was won by sufferings is proved by Prov. VI., 23. " Reproofs of instruction (i.e., sufferings) are the way of life." Sufferings are more potent than sacrifices to win God's favour, for sacrifices were rendered through money, but sufferings are rendered by the body.[34] Note how persistently sufferings are limited to mere bodily pain. The verse in Proverbs is quoted again and again. It was interpreted to mean not merely that him whom God loves He chastises, but that chastisements, or rather sufferings, produce the divine love. The sufferings of a man whom God loves are not in proportion to his deeds. Just because of His love, God sends the man more sufferings than he deserves.[35] For the Rabbis with their hereditary and ingrained tendency or desire to bring as much correspondence as they can into suffering and desert, this is a very bold and significant implication. It was, I suppose, only made possible to them by the doctrine of the future life. So, too, can the Rabbis refer the " very good " of the last day of creation (Gen. I., 31) to sufferings, because through them " the world to come " is obtained.[36] Hence it is that sufferings are to be regarded as the privilege of the righteous. Thus it is quaintly stated that God only chastises those whose hearts are as soft as lilies. If a man has two cows, one strong and one weak, upon which does he place the yoke? Upon the strong one. So God does not " try " the wicked, because they could not endure it; he tries the good. Or again: the flax merchant only beats good flax, which becomes the better for it. He does not beat the hard flax which would go to pieces. The potter does not beat porous pots, which would break. He beats good pots, which, however much he beats them, do not break. Even so God " tries " not the wicked, but the righteous.[37]

The view that sufferings purify is indicated in the comparison of them to salt. As salt makes meat fit to eat (lit: makes it sweet), so do sufferings destroy all sins. Here again the sufferings alluded to are predominantly physical pain, for, in the same passage, they are spoken of as crushing the whole human body. Because of this purifying effect of certain sufferings, a famous term was given to them: " sufferings of love." The primary Talmudic passage in which this term is employed deserves, in part, a literal quotation. It ends with the simile of the salt and with the " three good gifts " that I have already mentioned.

" Raba, others say, R. Chisda, said, If sufferings come to a man, let him examine his deeds; if he finds nothing blameworthy, the cause may be neglect of the study of the Law; if this also is not the case, then they (the sufferings) are chastisements of love, in accordance with the saying in Proverbs. As R. Huna said, Him in whom God takes pleasure He crushes with sufferings. (Isaiah LIII., 10). Lest we might suppose that this is so even if a man does not receive them in love, it is also said, If he make his soul an offering for sin (Isaiah LIII., 10); for as the sin offering must be offered willingly, so must sufferings be accepted willingly. If a man so receives them, what is his reward? He shall see his seed and live long (Isaiah LIII., 10). And not only that, but his study of the Law will be established. R. Jacob b. Idi said, Those are sufferings of love by which the study of the Law is not impeded."[38]

Curious and naïve is the statement: " The pious men of old were wont to be attacked by sufferings of the bowels about twenty days before their death, in order to destroy all their sins, and so that they might enter the world to come in purity."39 Not less odd is the following. R. Isaac comments upon the words in Ecclesiastes (VII., 27), " One by one, to make up the account," as follows. " A man commits a sin, for which the punishment is death by judgment of God. How is it atoned? His ox dies; his hen is lost; his vessel is broken; he knocks his little finger, and a drop of blood issues from it. So one thing is added to another, and the reckoning is made up."40

If therefore sufferings are, in so many cases, the result, not of God's enmity, but of His love, should they not be received, in full resignation and even with gladness? The Rabbis, though of some it is frankly recorded that they found the doctrine hard, taught it with marked insistence. And here they advance a considerable way beyond the Biblical level. Thus R. Akiba said, " The words in Exodus XX., 33, imply that the Israelites are not to deal with God as the nations deal with their gods. For they, when good befalls them, honour their gods, when evil befalls them, they curse, but God bids the Israelites give thanks when He sends them good, and give thanks also when He sends them sufferings. A man should rejoice in his sufferings more than in his prosperity, for it is the sufferings which bring about the forgiveness of his sins. So Moses said to the Israelites, If you accept your sufferings in joy, you shall receive your reward."41 The teaching is incorporated into the Mishnah. It becomes a law. " A man must bless God for the evil as well as for the good ; thou shalt love God with all thy soul means even if He take thy soul away. Thou shalt love God with all thy might means, Thou shalt love Him for every measure which He metes out to thee."42 (The Hebrew words for " might " and " measure " have a similar assonance). Sufferings are to be received, as it says, in another place and in a very peculiar context, in silence and in prayer.43 He who rejoices in his sufferings, says R. Joshua b. Levi, brings salvation into the world.44 The Midrash speaks of four ways in which sufferings can be received : these four ways are ascribed to four Biblical characters. The first way is that of Job who kicked and complained. The second is that of Abraham who laughed. The third way is that of Hezekiah who besought. The fourth (and highest) way is that of David, who said, " Why hangs the strap? Beat me with it."45 To this day in the orthodox prayer books the blessing is fixed for good tidings, " Blessed art thou, O Lord our God, King of the Universe, who art good and dispensest good," and for evil tidings, " Blessed art thou, O Lord our God, King of the

Universe, the true Judge (or Judge of Truth.") These blessings are taken direct from the Mishnah.[46] And Raba said that the special phraseology of the blessing for "evil" was merely to indicate that one must receive the evil in joy. Psalm CII., is used to prove that whether "judgment" befall a man or "lovingkindness," he must equally "sing." A similar use is made of Psalm LVI., 10., where, as is frequent with the Rabbis and with Philo, Elohim, or God, stands for the Divine Being in His aspect as the dispenser of judgment or justice, Yahweh, or the Lord, in His aspect as the dispenser of mercy and love. Or again, Psalm CXVI., 3, 4, 13, proves the same thing. For when I receive the cup of salvation (i.e., prosperity), I call upon the name of the Lord; when trouble and sorrow overtake me, I call upon the name of the Lord.[47] The happy ingenuity of the Rabbis, and their marvellously ready use of (because of their absolute familiarity with) the text of the Scriptures, are prettily illustrated by this devout acceptance of sorrow, by the joyous equivalence of good and evil in their attitude to God.

The highest form of chastisement or suffering is martyrdom. To bless God with all your soul even when He "takes" your soul in pain and torture—that is fulfilling the duty of blessing God for the "evil" as well as for the good in the noblest possible degree. If you love God then, you will love Him always; you are a true lover and a tried. The sufferings and persecutions which attended and followed the Hadrianic revolt made a deep impression upon the Jews in more ways than one. And it may be truly said that in some important respects it is Hadrian and Bar Kochba, who mark the close of one period and the opening of another, rather than the fall of Jerusalem and the destruction of the Temple. For all time the Jews looked back upon the death of Akiba as the supreme exemplification of the martyr's love for God and of his trust in the Divine Goodness. In one passage of the Midrash the chastisements of Israel are said to be divided into three equal parts, of which one part comprises those that will usher in the Messianic age, a second those which befell the Jews in the days of Hadrian, and the third includes all others at all other times both past and present.[48] The estimate of the volume of suffering endured in the age of the Great Revolt is thus clearly indicated. The words, "They that love me and keep my commandments," were applied to the martyrs. And the questions are put, Why goest thou forth to be executed by the sword? Because I circumcised my son, echoes the reply. Why goest thou forth to be burnt? Because I studied the Law.

Why goest thou forth to be scourged? Because I held the Lulab. Why goest thou forth to be crucified? Because I ate unleavened bread in its season. The words in Zechariah XIII., 6, are cleverly interpreted to mean, The chastisements which I received made me beloved by my Father who is in heaven.[49] Memories of those awful days provoked the remark, " If a man say to thee, give up thy life for the Sanctification of the Name, answer, I will do so; only may I be killed at once and not tortured as in the days of Hadrian."[50] Certain it was that those who gave and give their lives for the Sanctification of the Name would obtain the blessedness of " the world to come." The sons of the living God loved Him even unto death. That is the meaning of " sick of love " in the Song of Solomon. They were sick, not by pain of head or body, but by love of the Holy One—yea sick of love, even unto death. For the son so loves his Father that he gives up his life for the honour of his Father. Even as Shadrach, Meshach and Abednego gave their lives, not on the condition of rescue, but to be burnt, for it is said, " stronger than death is love."[51] More precious to me, God is made to say, than all sacrifices is the blood of the martyrs, who died for the Sanctification of my Name.[52] Akiba's end is justly famous. He fulfilled what was said by Eleazer, the Maccabean martyr, " In my body I endure sore pains; but in my soul I gladly suffer them for my fear of God." But to Akiba the fear was transfigured into love. " When Akiba was being tortured, the hour for saying the Shema arrived. He said it and smiled. The Roman officer called out, Old man, art thou a sorcerer, or dost thou mock at thy sufferings that thou smilest in the midst of thy pains? Neither, replied Akiba, but all my life, when I said the words, Thou shalt love the Lord thy God with all thy heart and might and soul, I was saddened, for I thought, when shall I be able to fulfil the command? I have loved God with all my heart and with all my possessions; but how to love Him with all my soul (i.e., life) was not assured to me. Now that I am giving my life, and that the hour for saying the Shema has come, and my resolution remains firm, should I not laugh? And as he spoke his soul departed."[53]

So far these palliations or transfigurations of suffering have been for the sake of him who suffers. But the Rabbis, though they did not use the doctrine of the Suffering Servant adequately, yet habitually taught that the death of the righteous atones for the sins of others. In a generation, it is said, in one well known passage, in which righteous men exist, they are taken away for the sins of their age, and when they do not exist, then the children are taken away.[54] In another passage Moses asks God what would happen to the Israelites if a time came when there was neither Tabernacle nor Temple; what would be their pledge? [There is an untranslatable play upon words between Dwelling (Tabernacle) and Pledge.] God replies that He will take away (i.e., remove by death) a righteous man from among them, and make him their pledge, and forgive them all their sins.[54a] Referring to Ezekiel IV., 4, it is said elsewhere: " If a locality rebels against an earthly king, he, if he be cruel, kills the whole population; if he be merciful, he kills only a half; if he be exceedingly merciful, he only punishes the great ones of the place; even so did God chastise Ezekiel to destroy the sins of Israel."[55] But the idea of this vicarious suffering is not ethically worked out. It remains a mere outward substitution; a mere remission of punishment. The Rabbis did not grasp and carry forward the conception of the Servant: a voluntary acceptance of suffering for the sake of others, and the moral improvement and purification of those others through, or because, or as a result of, that voluntary pain. That is a true palliative of suffering and a true consolation; we do not, so far as I am aware, come across it in the Rabbinical literature.

On the whole, too, it is rather striking that there seem to be so few allusions in the vast Rabbinical literature to sufferings which do not, as it were, fall directly upon the subject himself. The " yesurin " (chastisements, punishments, sufferings, as we may variously render the word) are illnesses, pains, tortures, or finally death, undergone by the sufferer. They seem very rarely to refer to those other sufferings, which are so poignant precisely because they are the sufferings of another—when that other is beloved. Consolations for this kind of suffering seem seldom attempted. Even for the death of those we love there seems (so far as I can find) to be little offered by way of comfort. We all know the famous story of Beruria, the wife of Rabbi Meir. " R. Meir was in Synagogue one Sabbath afternoon, and gave a discourse. While he was there, his two sons died. Their mother laid their bodies on the bed, and covered them with a cloth. At the expiration of the Sabbath R. Meir returned home. He said, ' Where are my two sons?' ' They went to the Synagogue,' she replied. ' I did not see them there,' he said. Then she gave him the Cup to make the blessing (at the close of the Sabbath). He said again, ' Where are my sons?' She said, ' Both went to a certain place and have now returned.' She then served to him his food. After he had said the blessing, she said, ' Master, I have a question to ask.' ' Ask,' he replied. She said, ' To-day before dawn a man came, and gave me something to keep for him : now he is about to return to take it back. Shall we give it back to him or not?' ' My daughter,' replied R. Meir, ' must not he who has received something from another for its safe preserval, give it back to its owner?' She said, ' Without your assent I would not give it back.' Then she took his hand, and led him up to the chamber, and brought him to the bed, and removed the cloth, and he saw his sons lying dead upon the bed. Then he began to weep, and to cry out, ' My sons, my sons.' Then she said to him, ' Did you not say that we must return what is lent to us to its owner? Did not Job say, the Lord has given, the Lord has taken?' Thus she comforted her husband and quieted him.''

It is a pity that to this charming tale the Midrash adds the stupid remark (sinking from the level of Job to that of his friends), '' Of what had R. Meir's sons been guilty that they both died at once? They were wont to rest in the Synagogue and to eat and drink there.''[56]

An earlier parallel to the story about Beruria is found in the story of the visit of the disciples of R. Jochanan b. Zakkai on the death of his son. The first said, '' Adam had a son who died, and yet Adam received consolation, as it is said, And Adam knew his wife again. So do you receive consolation.'' R. Jochanan replied, '' Not enough that I grieve for my own sorrow, but you remind me of Adam's sorrow !'' The second said, '' Job had sons and daughters, and they all died on one day, yet he received consolation, for he said, The Lord gave, the Lord has taken away.'' Jochanan replied, '' Not enough that I grieve for my own sorrow, but you would remind me of Job's sorrow.'' The third said, ''Aaron had two grown sons, and they died on one day, yet he received consolation, as it is said, And Aaron held his peace. So do you receive consolation.'' Jochanan replied, '' Not enough that I grieve for my own sorrow, but you would remind me of the sorrow of Aaron?'' The fourth said, '' King David had a son who died, and he received consolation, as is said, and David comforted Bathsheba and went in unto her. So do you receive consolation.'' Jochanan replied, '' Not enough that I grieve for my own sorrow, but you would remind me of the sorrow of David !'' Then R. Eleazer drew near to R. Jochanan, and when the latter saw him, he said to his servant, Take my clothes and follow me to the bath, for this is a great

man, and I cannot appear before him (in this condition). R.
Eleazer then entered, and sat down, and said to R. Jochanan,
" I will tell you a parable. The circumstances may be compared
with that of a man who received from the King an object to-
keep. Day by day the man used to weep, and cry, and say, When
shall I restore this trust unimpaired? So you, O Master, had a
son who had studied the Law and the Prophets and the Writings, who knew the Mishnah, and the Halachot, and the Agadah;
he was removed from this world without sin. Do you, therefore,
receive the consolation that you have given back your trust unimpaired." Then R. Jochanan said, " You have comforted me,
my son, as men are wont to comfort one another."[57]

On the deeper questions as to the origin of evil we obtain
little enlightenment from the Rabbis. Beyond the simple consolations which have so far been noted, they hardly go. A remark
of an otherwise little known Rabbi was incorporated in the Sayings of the Fathers, and has become very familiar. " Neither the
security of the wicked nor the afflictions of the righteous are in
our hand," in other words, we are unable to answer the questions: Why do the wicked flourish? Why do the righteous
suffer?[58] We have to accept with resignation the inscrutable will
of God. " When the angels asked God, why didst thou punish
Adam with death?, God replied, I enjoined a light command upon
him, and he transgressed it. But why, then, they said, did Moses
and Aaron, who kept the whole law, die? God answered, One
event happens alike to the righteous and the wicked." (Ecc. IX.,
2). Thus God puts them off. Far more dramatic is the famous
story of Akiba's vision. Moses is told by God of Akiba's wond-
rous knowledge, and how he will teach heaps and heaps of
injunctions (Halachot). Moses asks to see him, and is vouch-
safed a vision of Akiba and his students. After some further
conversation, Moses says to God, Thou hast shown me his
knowledge of the law; show me now his reward. Then the
vision changes, and Moses sees Akiba's flesh being weighed in
the butcher's shop. Then Moses says, " For such knowledge
of the law, is *this* the reward? Silence, replies God; so I have
determined." There must be no cavil at God's degree.[58a] As
the Rabbis do not clearly distinguish between physical evil
and moral evil, it is not surprising that they should not come to
grips with the supreme problems, what is the origin, and what is
the purport, of sin? In their many remarks upon the Yetzer ha
Ra, the evil impulse—interesting, novel and suggestive as they
are—we do not find any elaborate and consistent body of doctrine

upon the more difficult portions of the subject. Dr. Porter, in his valuable study, truly observes, "The Rabbis did not grapple in a fundamental, philosophical way with the difficulty involved in the goodness of God and the evil disposition of man as God made him. . . . We cannot indeed blame them for not solving a problem which no one has solved, but their discussions of it often seem more like play than like serious and worthy labour."59

The Rabbis, in their simple faith that God by His free choice and will created everything, usually ascribed to Him too the creation of the Yetzer. In that sense He is responsible, as creator, for human sin. But if we then ask: why did He create it, we receive from the Rabbis no clear reply. Yet we do find certain answers which suggest theories that were germinating in their minds. It is, for instance, indicated (though not expressed) that, for purposes hidden from view, God created man with his frailty and liability to sin in order that, with the divine help, he might, both as an individual and as a race, triumph over the weakness, and reach the higher blessedness of victory. The Law is God's antidote to the Yetzer. Thus "God has given the Yetzer to us that by overcoming it we may receive reward."60 In the Messianic Age upon earth, and in the world to come beyond the grave, the Yetzer will be destroyed. A more profound, though not by any means fully worked out view, (not wholly inconsistent with the former) was that the Yetzer was somehow necessary for man's development. The very "impulse" which might be the cause of the vilest and most terrible sins might also be the cause of necessary and desirable activities. It was doubtless the sexual life which suggested this idea.* Marriage is honourable and (to the Rabbinic view) far higher than virginity: the sexual impulse is its root. Yet this same impulse can be "developed" into license, unchastity and sin. Thus we get the fine conception of the sanctification of the natural instincts: the taming of the Yetzer into a servant, which may result in human progress and the glory of God. Thus a certain Rabbi, in a well-known passage, goes so far as to declare that the evil Yetzer is very

---

* In the strange Rabbinic legend, quoted in Porter, p. 120 (Yoma 69b), the Yetzer of unchastity is delivered up to the Israelites. "The prophet said to them, If you kill it, the world will cease. They bound it for three days, and when they searched for a new laid egg in all the land of Israel, they found none. Then they said, What shall we do? If we pray for a half, we know that heaven gives no halves. So they put out its eyes, and let it go, and this profited at least so much that men are no longer incited to incest."

good. How can this be? It is very good because, without it, no man would build a house, or marry, or beget children, or engage in trade.[61] Yet the same Yetzer is the cause of all business cheating and sexual iniquity. Tame the Yetzer, and it will become a servant for good. Man has both good and bad impulses—a good Yetzer as well as an evil Yetzer. So it is said that even as a man who has two cows, one of which is good for ploughing and one bad, if he wants to use the bad one, puts the yoke on both, so should we join the evil impulse to the good, and use it in the right way. As iron is made useful by fire, so the evil Yetzer is made serviceable by the Law.[62] Very significant is the injunction in the Mishnah that man is to love God with the evil Yetzer as well as with the good.[63] The idea appears to be that every conceivable faculty and instinct and impulse of man are to be devoted to the divine service, and concentrated upon the love of God. It is a paradox; yet it means that the ideal is the unification of man's whole nature in a sustained and intensive love of his divine Master. A certain Rabbinic legend, too long to quote here, seems to imply the view that sin itself is the result of a lack of complete faith and confidence in God. Had the Israelites put nothing between them and God—perhaps could man now put nothing between him and God, could his faith be absolute—the evil impulse would be wholly overcome.[64]

There are certain modern comforts which mean much to some people and nothing to others, of which, according to Dr. Schechter, there are adumbrations in Rabbinical literature. How far is God Himself engaged in a conflict with evil? Or if not engaged in a conflict, how far is His omnipotence limited by the very ends which He has set before Himself to achieve? There are a few Rabbinical passages which, in Dr. Schechter's opinion, "hint at the possibility that even God's omnipotence is submitted to a certain law—though designed by His own holy will—which He could not alter without detriment to the whole creation. . . We read of a certain renowned Rabbi, who lived in great poverty, that once in a dream he asked the divine Shechinah how long he would still have to endure this bitter privation." This is the story. "R. Eleazer of Pedath was in great straits of poverty. He was bled, and had nothing to eat. He took the peel of some garlic, and put it in his mouth, and his heart grew faint, and he slept. The Rabbis came to ask him a question. They saw him weep and laugh, and a ray of fire came out of his forehead. When he awoke, they asked him, why did you weep and laugh? He said, the Holy One sat by me, and I asked Him how long I should be distressed in this world. He replied, Eleazar, my son, would it please you (or would it seem right to you) that I should over-turn the world from the beginning (i.e., begin the creation anew), that you might perhaps be born in an hour of food (i.e., plenty)?"[64a] Whether, however, God is subject to these limita-tions or no (and many of us would now-a-days say that He is), one may raise the further question whether He, too, suffers in the inevitable suffering of His creation. This thought, too, gives comfort to some, and means little or nothing to others. Thus Dr. Carpenter, the eminent Unitarian scholar and divine, in alluding to the "nameless souls in inconspicuous places who have carried the burden of the world's struggles, infirmities, and sins, mutilated by accident, wasted by disease,—the innumerable multitude of those upon whose toil the fabric of our civilization has been reared," observes: " Their sufferings, though hid from man, are known to God; and, I will add, according to my faith, he shares them, too; for he in whom we live and move and have our being feels in our nerves and understands our pain, and the long passion of our humanity is borne in all its multitudinous variety by him. I do not say that this conception relieves every difficulty, but it lifts the whole process on to another plane. God is no longer a mere outside spectator; he is the companion, if he is also (in part at least) the author, of our woe."[64b]

The Rabbis do not go so far as this. Yet, in a more simple and pictorial way, they go near it. It is a favourite thought with them that God, or the Shechinah, suffers with the suffering of Israel. That strange verse in Isaiah (lxiii. 9) (of which the text is probab'y corrupt), "in all their affliction He was afflicted," they make much use of. As Dr. Schechter observes: "God is repre-sented as mourning for seven days (as in the case when one loses a child) before He brought the deluge on the world : He bemoans the fall of Israel and the destruction of the Temple, and the Shechinah laments even when the criminal suffers his just pun-ishment." The last allusion is very remarkable: it occurs, moreover, in the Mishnah (Sanhedrin, vi. 5; 46a). "R. Meir said, when a man suffers pain (i.e., when a criminal is executed), what does the Shechinah say? ' Heavy is my head, heavy is my arm !' If God grieves so much over the blood of the wicked, how much more over the death of the righteous." Strangest, and not, perhaps, least significant, of these Talmudic passages is one to which Dr. Schechter also calls attention. Two Rabbis pass the ruined house of a third Rabbi who had been very rich and very benevolent. The first Rabbi sighs. His companion asks him the reason. He replies: "How should I not sigh? Here was a house in which 60 bakers by day and 60 by night baked for all who had need, and the owner never took his hand from his purse, for he said, Perchance a poor man of good family may come, and he might be ashamed to wait till I fetch my purse ; and here, moreover, four doors stood open to the four quarters of the world, and every one who went in hungry came out satisfied, and here in years of famine wheat and barley were put outside, so that every one who was ashamed to take by day came and took by night—and now this house is in ruins! Should I not sigh?" After some further conversation the second Rabbi perceived that the mind of the first Rabbi was still not quieted. Whereupon he uttered these brief and pregnant words: "It is enough for the servant to be as his Master." The Master is God, and the idea is that since God suffers, man need not, and should not, complain.[64c]

It must be admitted that many of our modern perplexities are ignored and unnoticed by the Rabbis. They do not adequately distinguish, as we have seen, between physical suffering and moral suffering, between the suffering that ennobles and the suffering that degrades, between voluntary suffering and involuntary, between the suffering that comes to me as the result of my sin, or as the result of another's sin, or as the result of both, or of neither. Again, the perplexities which arise from the relation of God to evil, whether physical or moral, are not fully realised. They do not perceive the full difficulty in ascribing evil to the causation of God, or of denying that evil *is* evil just because all things are supposed to come from God, or because God is believed to be omnipotent. Again, the wicked are to them a problem only, so far as they are prosperous and injure the good: they are hardly yet a problem in themselves, so that the sheer destruction of the wicked becomes really a graver puzzle than the calamity of the good. And the paradox of nothing being good but virtue and the good will is neither affirmed nor denied. Yet the fine faith of the Rabbis can still help us. We can still be stirred by their confidence in the divine righteousness, the divine love. We can still admire the Rabbinic ideal of those who are " humiliated and do not humiliate, who hear reproaches and do not answer them, who fulfil the commands in love, and rejoice in their afflictions," we can still value that high passion for God which could make one of them say that the daughter of Israel speaks before God, and says, " Lord of the world, even though my Beloved oppresses and embitters me,

yet shall He lie between my breasts." No sorrow and no affliction, however mysterious, however grievous, shall interrupt the
close communion of man with God.[65]

And, upon the whole, the joy of that communion sufficed to
keep the Israelites of the Rabbinic age buoyant in the midst of
trouble; their spirits were unquenched by persecution. They
remained optimists to the end, and declared as, on the whole,
their descendants still declare, that even this life on earth is God's
gift, and that even this life on earth is good.

It is curious to see what the Midrash makes of, and how it
interprets, the one pessimistic book in the Hebrew Scriptures.
See, for example, how it deals with the famous saying, " The
day of death is better than the day of birth." The saying is in
the Sacred Scriptures; it is so clear that it could hardly be explained away. But it is given an ethical interpretation, which
turns it into something very different from its original meaning,
or from Herodotus' story about the Trausians that I quoted
before. " When a child is born, all rejoice; when a man dies,
all weep. But in truth we should not rejoice when a child is
born, for one knows not *if he will be good or bad, righteous or
wicked;* when a man dies, one should rejoice that he has departed from the world *with a good name and in peace.* One ship
sailed out from the harbour; one ship put into the harbour. Men
rejoiced over the first, but not over the second. A wise man said
that one should rather refrain from rejoicing over the ship which
leaves the harbour, for one knows not how many seas and
tempests it will encounter; but over the ship which has returned
to port one should rejoice that it has returned in peace. So
should we rejoice over the dead who have departed from the
world in peace." But it would not have been possible for these
words to have been written except for the belief that the port of
death is the entrance to another life, or, as it says in this same
passage, " When a man is born, he may be numbered among the
dying, when he has died, he may be numbered among the
living."[66]

Here I have to break off. It would be very interesting, were
a real scholar to take up the story at this point, and to delineate
the comforts and consolations offered by Jewish writers and
thinkers from the close of the Rabbinic era to modern times.
How far did new points of view emerge? What fresh conceptions of comfort were put forward? How far were the old consolations retained, and how far were they modified? How far
was the stress shifted from one doctrine to another? And how

far were new palliatives offered for newly discovered difficulties and problems? There would be room indeed here for a study which, so far as I know, has never been attempted, and would surely be of great theoretic interest, and perhaps, too, of much practical advantage. Will no real scholar, in the spirit of true impartiality and of plain historic objectivity, attempt the task?

Meanwhile, before passing on to the second portion of my own limited field, it may be well to reflect for a moment upon what has thus far been obtained. We may, I think, truly say that the two great consolations achieved are, (1) the doctrine of the One and Only God, perfect in wisdom and goodness, greatly caring for His people and for man, and (2) the doctrine of a future life. From these two doctrines corollaries are drawn, as that there is a purpose in human history, and a purpose in human suffering. If we roughly compare the Rabbinic position with our own, we find (as I have already observed) that their difficulties are in some respects less than ours and in some respects greater. Smaller knowledge and restricted experience hid from their eyes torturing problems which stare us all too obviously in the face. And, beyond these, a more penetrating dialectic, a more searching scepticism, have made us perceive difficulties where our ancestors did not perceive them, or realise the inadequacy and unsoundness of explanations and solutions, in which they were able to find strength and comfort. It is needless to make a catalogue of these difficulties. Some have already been mentioned. On the other hand, certain troubles worry us less than they worried them. We also, it is true, are perplexed by the calamities of the righteous, yet we are less perplexed by them than they were. Or is it that we have found some better solutions or palliatives? We are less concerned about the relation of prosperity to desert ; we insist far less upon the value and divineness of the doctrine of exact retribution. We distinguish more clearly between moral and physical evil, between the calamity of sin and the calamity of pain ; between the suffering of the body and the disease of the soul. If we witness a life which has been ennobled both by involuntary suffering and by voluntary self-sacrifice, we do not *merely* hold that a consolation and a palliative of these pains and sorrows are to be found in the fact that the soul has been purified and made fit for a life of beatitude in the hereafter, but we consider that the noble life and its influence and its activities have a value in themselves and even a " reward " in themselves, and that here too is a consolation and

here too is a palliative. And we also, I think, lay more stress
upon the cosmic side of our human activities—even though man
and his planet have become a mere speck in the infinite universe.
We believe that, somehow or other, the greatness of man has a
universal value, and is connected with the universal order and
with the divine existence, operation and rule. Human love,
human righteousness, human self-sacrifice, are not only a blessing to humanity: they are—so upon our vision it flashes—a
blessing to the universe and to God.

Do the Greeks contribute anything of value to the thought
and literature of consolation? To the literature surely: for they
clothe ethical commonplaces in noble language. And also to the
thought. For even supposing that we meet in all their writings
from Homer to Epictetus no consoling thought to which we do
not find a parallel in Biblical or Rabbinic literature, yet the
stress may not always be the same. A thought may be central
to the Greeks which is only occasional to the Hebrew; or the
very difference of accent may give a peculiar interest to the
parallel. The same conception will wear a difference of *nuance*
as expressed by Hebrew and by Greek, and hence each expression may possess its own particular value. But there are Greek
thoughts which are more than parallels; their originality is
higher than a difference in accent or expression. We may even
legitimately say that some of the added palliatives and consolations of to-day were prepared or foreshadowed by the Greeks.

Our main attention is to be paid to a very late chapter in
Greek literature, and one, perhaps, least purely and genuinely
Greek: perhaps for that very reason it can most appropriately be
placed side by side with our *florilegium* from the Bible and the
Talmud. That late chapter is formed by such fragments of the
Stoic philosophers as have survived for us, and more especially
by the words of Epictetus, the slave, and Marcus Aurelius, the
Emperor. And it may be that the peculiar passion and fervour
of the Stoics, whereby they are still masters in austere consolation even to the modern world, is partly due to the Eastern
origin of Zeno, the founder, and of many writers of his school.
But before we speak of these Stoics and of their teaching, there
is something to be said of the Greeks of the earlier ages, and
something of ethical value (and not only of beauty) to be reaped
and garnered even from them.

We must not, indeed, expect too much. The Greeks were no
monotheists in our sense of the word ; even to such a profoundly
religious mind as Aeschylus or Sophocles, Zeus was not the lov-

ing Father, " the Lord, the Lord, merciful, long-suffering, for-giving," which He was to the Biblical and Talmudic writers, or which He is to ourselves. An intimacy of religious communion between God and the individual man must not be sought for from the Greeks. And, perhaps, too, just because God was less near and less loving, whether to the nation or to the individual, less was expected from Him; and there was less complaint when things went wrong and calamity befell. So far as God or the gods are not perfectly good, so far as He or they are not all powerful or all righteous, the ethical sting in suffering and evil is less severe. The clash of emotions is less poignant, and certainly less interest-ing. An attack upon, or a complaint against, a God who is not *ex hypothesi,* and *ex professo,* perfect in justice and goodness, is remote from our own thought. It raises no moral difficulty, and demands no ethical explanation.

But, on the other hand, the fact that the Greeks demanded less of God or of the gods produced effects of value. For it threw them back upon themselves, and it made them seek for comfort from life as it was rather than from life as it ought to be. They worried far less than the Hebrews (which does not mean that they did not worry at all) over the unequal relation of circum-stance to desert : they were occupied much less than the Hebrews in praying for their own salvation and happiness and for the overthrow and destruction of their foes. If, indeed, they had been ordinary people, then the comfort which they could have drawn from life as it was would not have been to us of interest or value. But they were not ordinary people. The chosen few among them, at any rate, were men of extraordinary genius and insight, and thus the comfort they drew from life was not the mere passing comfort of the senses (no mere " let us eat and drink, for to-morrow we die "), but the comfort of all that makes life great and glorious through the mind and the will. If, for instance, it may be said that to the Greeks virtue was its own reward, this was not the final result of high ethical teaching, but it was due to the conviction that certain sorts of virtue (for example, courage and self-sacrifice in war) were desirable and beautiful in themselves. The deeds they prompted were precious and delightful, not for their results (except perchance the result of fame and glory), but in the doing, and at the time. Glorious activities of body and mind were valuable in themselves; they did not need, and they did not necessarily obtain, any requital or reward. This feeling of joy and value in the doing or in the being doubtless required a spiritual deepening, such as it received in Plato and the Stoics, but the deepening could hardly have happened without it. And we may, I think, regard it as the source, or at any rate, as one source, of our own profoundest appreciation of righteousness and wisdom and love not for their results, but for themselves.

The intellectual capacity, the openeyedness and sanity of the Greeks, or of the higher spirits among them, enabled them to look at life with calm discrimination. They had an acute sense both of joy and of sorrow. Nothing is falser than to think of them as light-hearted. A profound undertone of melancholy pervades their writings from Homer onwards. In no literature can we find more emphatic utterances concerning the sadness and miseries of human existence: frequently is the saying repeated in various forms that the best thing is not to be born at all, and the second best to die as soon as possible.⁶⁷ Yet in spite of exclamations such as these, the joys of life, physical, mental, moral, were keenly felt, realized, appreciated. Sometimes the one were set off or balanced against the other, and in view of life's extreme uncertainty, the advice of the moralist was neither to be too joyful in prosperity nor too grieved in misfortune. "Rejoice," so runs a fragment of the poet Archilochus, " in what is delightful, and be not over vexed at ill: recognise the rhythm that holds men (i.e., recognise the balance of life.")⁶⁸ It seemed to the Greeks no use to grumble too much at miseries which man is powerless to avoid or to overthrow. So far as they come from the gods, complaint is idle, for the gods are far stronger than man; so far as they are entwined, and inseparably connected, with the ultimate order of the world, to which even the gods are subject, they are clearly inevitable; only so far as they are man's own fault—the result of sin, folly and insolence—is their cure within human power. The man of sense and education, the man of intellectual insight and moral strength will realise this most clearly. Therefore to the Greeks to endure bravely is the mark of a noble mind. " Endure" says Ulysses to his own soul. Endurance is his characteristic and his virtue. And if the fates have sent many woes to man, they have at least given him an enduring soul with which to bear them. The man of noble nature does not refuse to bear the blows of heaven. Such unavoidable ills must be borne with resignation, as the ills which are inflicted by a human enemy with courage. So Pericles admonishes the Athenians, when the plague and the war lay heavy upon them. " The greatest men and the greatest states, when misfortunes come, are the least depressed in spirit and the most resolute in action."[69] Even the somewhat gloomy and prudential Theognis says much the same. " No one is altogether happy. But the good man, nevertheless, endures his misfortune, and makes no show of it : the weakling knows neither how to attune his mind to good or ill. But as the gifts of the immortals are of all kinds, one must bear bravely and lightly what they send us."[70] So, too, in Pindar. " It is best to bear lightly the yoke that rests on one's neck." " The gods give to man two woes for every good : these woes foolish men cannot bear with grace, but the good know how to bear them by ever turning the fairer side to the front."[71] Thus the simplest Greek comfort was to impress upon the mind the compensations of life and the power of the soul to bear sorrows with fortitude. If sufferings are overcome, their very memory may be sweet. Or again, we find the reflection, " Let us not remember evils when we have good things in our hand." This saying is put by Herodotus into the mouth of Xerxes in reply to his uncle, who had struck a note of deepest pessimism, and the king adds " It is better to have courage about everything, and to suffer half the evils which threaten, than to have fear beforehand about everything and not to suffer any evil at all."[72] Life, at any rate, to the brave, is something of a glorious adventure. But, on the other hand, an insensibility to affliction is also not the ideal—certainly not to a Greek of the classic period, and perhaps the point of view of their most characteristic utterances would be expressed in the saying of Seneca, " non sentire mala sua non est hominis, et non ferre non est viri." It is not human not to feel afflictions, it is manly to endure them.[73]

But did the Greeks know any further consolation than that of sheer fortitude and endurance? I will not touch upon the special consolations of the mystics, or of those who believed in a future life of happiness and beatitude. Let us confine ourselves to the generality, for whom this life was the only sure scene of joy and achievement. Gloomy, if beautiful, are the words of the nurse in the Hippolytus of Euripides; yet they probably reflect what many a Greek felt about life and death : " Man's whole life is full of anguish; no respite from his woes he finds : but if there is ought to love beyond this life, night's dark pall wraps it round. And so we show our mad love of this life, because its light is shed on earth, and because we know no other, and have nought revealed to us of all our earth may hide." Yet the Greeks sometimes achieved a better comfort than the nurse could give to Phaedra in her sore sickness. " Be of good heart, dear child, toss not so wildly to and fro. Lie still, be brave, so wilt thou find thy sickness easier to bear; suffering for mortals is necessity."[74] There was, as I have said, the comfort of noble deeds, which are beautiful in themselves and desirable for their own sake. Even as early as Homer we find this thought pretty fully developed. Sarpedon expresses it in his speech to Glaukos in the battlefield. " Ah, friend, if once escaped from this battle we were for ever to be ageless and immortal, neither would I fight myself in the foremost ranks, nor would I send thee into the war that giveth man renown, but now—for assuredly ten thousand fates of death do every way beset us, and these no mortal may escape or avoid—now let us go forward, whether we shall give glory to other men, or others to us."[75] An aristocratic comfort, perhaps, but yet a comfort, and one capable of expansion. We find it again, expanded and generalised, many centuries after Homer in Demosthenes. " Seeing that a fixed term for all men is death, good men must attempt noble deeds, holding hope before them as their shield, and bearing what God sends them with resignation and courage."[76] There is something in man which drives him on to noble exploits, however dark and unknowable the future. Even as Pindar says: "From Zeus there comes no clear sign to men: yet we embark upon great endeavours, and yearn after many deeds; for by untameable hope our bodies are enthralled, but the tides of foreknowledge are hidden from our eyes."[77]

It may be asked, how far did the Greeks require comfort against the fact of death and in what did such comfort consist? And here, again, we will put aside all comforts which were obtained from the hope of any life of happiness beyond the grave. To most Greeks of the classical period, and even to most of the great men of that period, death is either the absolute end of consciousness, or the life of Hades, by which it is followed (like the life of Sheol to the Hebrews), is not in any wise worth the living.

Upon the whole, it would, I fancy, be true to say that the desire to live a *long* life upon earth,—to live to old age,—was considerably less great among the Greeks than among the Hebrews. " Whom the gods love die young " is not a saying which could have originated among the Hebrews. To the Hebrews, life was, or ought to be, a blessing from God, and if it was often full of pains and sorrows, yet in few of them, and in few of their greater writers, did these pains and sorrows deepen into a dislike and contempt of life as a whole, or even into a wish to be rid of it as soon as possible. They wanted to be rid of the pains and the sorrows, but not to be rid of life itself. Moreover, old age was, it would seem, a happier time among the Hebrews than among the Greeks. And ethically the Hebrews stood higher than the Greeks in their reverence for the old. A death, which prevented the mournful experiences and the sorry conditions which the Greeks seem, upon the whole, to associate with old age, could scarcely be looked upon as an unmixed evil.[78]

To the Greek, then, far more than to the Hebrew, death was in itself a consolation for the ills of life, whether for ills already experienced or for ills that might reasonably be expected. But both to Hebrew and to Greek the *manner* of death made a considerable difference, or, perhaps, it would be more correct to say, the period of life which immediately preceded death. It is doubtless characteristic of human nature all the world over to look to the end. Assume a life of gloom and oppression and unhappiness which lasts forty years, and assume further that the cloud lifts, and that for two years there is peace and happiness and recognition—the tendency is to consider that the two years have wiped out the forty. Reverse the conditions, and the tendency is just the same. The short period of happiness and recognition, the short period of misery and ruin (especially if it terminate in a sudden and painful death) wipe out, both as regards men's estimate of the character of the life as a whole and their estimate of divine justice in relation to that life, the long period which preceded. Men do not strike a balance : they do not regard the forty years of happiness or of misery as the dominant feature, or, subtracting the less amount from the greater, judge by the result. It is not the length which counts, but the order. If the few good years succeed the many bad ones, they make the difference, and if the few bad ones succeed the good ones, they give to the whole its character and its assessment. As the end is so important and conclusive in human eyes, so it is made conclusive and important in the eyes of God. This, at least, is what we find (as we have already observed) among the Hebrews. For calamity at the end and a miserable death meant to them either a divine judgment or, on the other hand, it seemed to mean a divine injustice. Hence the frequent assertions of the awful " end " of the wicked. Such an end was not merely desired as a punishment of the enemy : it was desired as a vindication of God. And the happy end, the peaceful death in old age, was desired, not mainly as a mere human happiness, but as a public evidence of righteousness, a proof of the divine justice.

Both " ends " satisfied. They wiped out the memories of previous
undeserved misfortune. They secured God's acquittal in the
forum of the heart. All must die: but in the manner of death
could lie its comfort. Thus the orthodox Eliphaz consoles Job by
telling him that his sorrows shall end in happiness: " he shall
come to his grave in a full age, as a shock of corn is brought in
in its season."[79] And, as we have already heard, Job's bitterest
attack upon the divine justice lies in the undeserved contrast in
the manner of men's death, for whereas one man dies in the
bitterness of his soul, another, and a wicked man, spends long
years in prosperity, and goes down in peace unto Sheol.

To some extent the Greeks felt the same, though the doubt
as to divine justice worried them less, just because they believed
in it less thoroughly. Hence too they did not so much regard
the " end " as the proof of human wickedness or human
virtue, or feel such agony when it was impossible to argue from
the " end " to the character, or assimilate the character to the
" end." But they too laid great stress upon the " end " as the
real test of the happiness or misery of human life taken as a
whole. No saying is more famous or more familiar in their
literature than Solon's warning: " Call no man happy before he
dies." Its meaning (in spite of Aristotle's gentle criticism that
it is strange to have to wait to call a man happy till he is no
longer existent, for surely happiness implies life and activity),
plainly indicates the emphasis laid upon the end.[80] The fifth act
is the crucial act. Four acts of happiness and one of sorrow.
Four acts of sorrow and one of happiness. It is the last act which
gives to the five their character as a whole. And, therefore, it
is not merely long antecedent prosperity which is the comfort of
death: the comfort of death may come in the very act of death.
A glorious and noble death is its own comfort and its own reward.
Both adjectives are significant. The Greeks have helped us to
appreciate and find comfort in a noble death: but part of the
comfort to them consisted in that death being known and praised
and remembered. To die for one's country's sake is in itself a
comfort, but especially if death gave victory, and was followed
by fame. On the Athenians who died at Plataea Simonides'
epitaph ran thus: " If to die nobly is the chief part of excellence,
to us out of all men Fortune gave this lot; for hastening to set
a crown of freedom on Hellas, we lie possessed of praise that
grows not old." And upon the Lacedaemonian dead the epitaph
was: " These men having set a crown of imperishable glory on
their own land were folded in the dark cloud of death: yet being

dead they have not died, since from on high their excellence raises them gloriously out of the house of Hades."[81] In the somewhat arid and cold comfort (as it seems to us) which Pericles gives to the relations of the fallen dead in his great funeral speech, the words about honour and glory (even if it be a weakness) still appeal to us: " They may be deemed fortunate who have gained most honour, whether an honourable death like theirs, or an honourable sorrow like yours. . . . Remember " (thus he speaks to the older men) " that your life of sorrow will not last long, and be comforted by the glory of those who are gone. For the love of honour alone is ever young, and not riches, as some say, but honour is the delight of men when they are old and uselsss." And what Englishman, reading in 1916 or 1917 the words which follow, can read them unmoved? " I would have you day by day fix your eyes upon the greatness of Athens, until you become filled with the love of her; and when you are impressed by the spectacle of her glory, reflect that this empire has been acquired by men who knew their duty, and had the courage to do it, who in the hour of conflict had the fear of dishonour always present to them, and who, if ever they failed in an enterprise, would not allow their virtues to be lost to their country, but freely gave their lives to her as the fairest offering which they could present at her feast. The sacrifice which they collectively made was individually repaid to them; for they received again each one for himself a praise which grows not old, and the noblest of all sepulchres—I speak not of that in which their remains are laid, but of that in which their glory survives, and is proclaimed always and on every fitting occasion both in word and deed. For the whole earth is the sepulchre of famous men; not only are they commemorated by columns and inscriptions in their own country, but in foreign lands there dwells also an unwritten memorial of them, graven not in stone, but in the hearts of men."[82] To die in the hour of victory, that, says Xenophon, is the fairest end.[83] And the noble death was to the Greeks a comfort, not merely because it was noble and known, but because it *was* the end. No misfortune could mar it, no squalid misery could follow or dim its glory. Thus it was that Solon's story of Cleobis and Biton always retained its place in the Hellenic heart. They had enjoyed a simple and happy life, and finally had wrought a notable and noble deed, for when their mother desired greatly to attend a festival at a distant temple, and no oxen could be found, they yoked themselves to the cart and drew it five and forty furlongs to the goal. " Then after they had done this, and had been seen by the assembled crowd, there came to their life a most excellent ending; and in this the deity declared that it was better for man to die than to continue to live. For the Argive men were standing round and extolling the strength of the young men, while the Argive women were extolling the mother to whose lot it had fallen to have such sons; and the mother being exceedingly rejoiced both by the deed itself and by the report made of it, took her stand in front of the goddess, and prayed that she would give to Cleobis and Biton her sons, who had honoured her so greatly, that gift which it is best for man to receive: and after this prayer, when they had sacrificed and feasted, the young men lay down to sleep within the temple itself, and never rose again, but were held bound in this last end."[84] Solon's verdict that these young men were among the happiest of men greatly appealed to Hellenic sentiment. In a certain degree, surely, it also appeals to our own. If one can say, "Felix opportunitate mortis," that is a real comfort.

Apart from the philosophers, there is hardly much more " comfort " to be found among the Greeks. But it should be noticed that even as the Hebrews of the Biblical age already reached the palliative of the educational value of suffering, so too had the Greeks. "My sufferings," says Croesus in Herodotus, " have proved to be lessons of wisdom to me."[85] The assonance of the words shows a proverbial use. " Pathêmata mathêmata." Sorrows are instructions. Aeschylus, in a famous passage in the Agamemnon, speaks of Zeus as " the guider of mankind upon the path of understanding by ordinance of Instruction by Suffering as a law established. When sore pain, that puts in mind of suffering, breaks out before the heart in time of sleep, then sober thoughts come over the reluctant will: it is a forced kindness, I take it, of Powers enthroned upon an awful seat."[86] There is a wonderful fragment of Sophocles which says that " a mind cradled in misfortunes perceives many things."[87] Suffering reveals.

How far did the philosophers of Greece relieve that deep sense of life's sadness which was so widely prevalent? What consolations had they to add to the few we have already noticed? I put aside the great Stoics for the moment, for I must deal with them at greater length. But speaking generally of all the philosophers, it seems to me that their main contributions were these two. First, they drew a marked distinction between what we now call physical evil or physical good, and moral evil or moral good. Secondly, in accordance with that great distinction, they laid an immense stress upon moral good or moral evil in comparison with physical good or physical evil. I include in the word "moral good" all that we now call intellectual good. Moral or intellectual good consisted, as they held, in the well-being, and in the activities, of man's mind and will, and was to a large extent independent of physical good or physical evil. To a large extent the soul is capable of being its own master, and in what we call calamities and miseries its greatness, nay, even its well-being, can be manifested and developed. The profit of every excellence, whether moral or intellectual, lies in itself; the retribution of every voluntary or involuntary corruption of the soul or the mind lies also in itself. This doctrine by no means explains either the origin, the meaning, or the purpose of evil, and when the philosophers attempt any such explanation, they fail. But it is, I think, for all that a helpful doctrine, and within its limits it still conveys to us a measure of austere and fortifying comfort. To some considerable extent it gives an answer to that particular phase of the problem which was so poignantly distressing to the author of Job, to so many other Jewish writers, and to such innumerable Jewish hearts. For it throws a new light upon the old dogma of retribution, and so far as the wicked are concerned, it turns the dogma upside down. For the prosperity of the wicked becomes their punishment, while the calamity of the good is either their opportunity, or, at least, without relation to the independent excellence of their mind and soul. In Plato the doctrine is combined with, and given a metaphysical and theological support by, the doctrine of immortality.

It is unnecessary to transcribe here (and it would occupy too many pages) all those great passages in Plato wherein these teachings are laid down. A few of them I have copied out in my Bible for Home Reading, Vol. II., pp. 202-204. Doubtless Plato presses his teaching sometimes to the verge of paradox, but (unlike the Stoics) it is doubtful whether he ever definitely passes the boundary. Hence his noble words still fortify and console. For we are still susceptible to any appeal ,which bids us regard the soul and its excellence as the greatest possession of man, which asks us to make a sharp distinction between the "goods of the body" and the "goods of the soul." So far as the mere prosperity of the wicked is concerned, we may say that Plato has demolished that particular bogey for ever. For we agree with him "that the unjust or doer of unjust actions is

miserable in any case—more miserable, however, if he be not punished, and does *not* meet with retribution, at the hands of gods or of men." We too should agree that "the greatest penalty of evil doing is to grow into the likeness of bad men," or that " to do wrong is second only in the scale of evils; but to do wrong and not be punished is first and greatest of all." Plato does not emphasize so keenly as certain Stoics that suffering may be the opportunity of the good for superb exhibitions of fortitude, devotion, and self-sacrifice, that adversity is the school and training ground of character, but he is filled with the profound faith that no true evil can befall the good, and that, somehow or other, all things will turn out well for them in the end. " This then must be our notion of the just man, that even when he is in poverty or sickness or any other seeming misfortune, all things will in the end work together for good to him in life and death.⁸⁸

Many thoughts concerning the future destiny of the soul passed before the great mind of Plato, nor can we say that he rested in complete faith on any one of the different forms in which he represented the idea of immortality in his dialogues. But that the soul did not cease with the cessation of bodily life— of this he seems to have remained assured. So sometimes he clothes the idea in forms and myths, which to us seem distant and strange; and sometimes he adopts the doctrine of transmigration. One of the mythological tales about the fortunes of the soul after death he puts into the mouth of Socrates in his last conversation with his disciples just before he drinks the cup of poison. Socrates first proves the immortality or indestructibility of the soul by logical and metaphysical arguments that hardly appeal to us at the present time: he appends to these arguments his tale. And then in conclusion he adds the famous words: " A man of sense ought not to say, nor will I be very confident, that the description which I have given of the soul and of her mansions is exactly true. But I do say that, inasmuch as the soul is shown to be immortal, he may venture to think, not improperly or unworthily, that something of the kind is true. The venture is a glorious one, and he ought to comfort himself with words like these, which is the reason why I lengthen out the tale. Wherefore, I say, let a man be of good cheer about his soul, who having cast away the pleasures and ornaments of the body as alien to him and working harm rather than good, has sought after the pleasures of knowledge; and has arrayed the soul, not in some foreign attire, but in her own proper jewels, temperance, and justice, and courage, and nobility, and truth—

in these adorned she is ready to go on her journey to the world below, when her hour comes."[89]

Faith of this kind we do not meet with in Aristotle. To him indeed there is no continued individual consciousness or recollection of the past after death. Yet from his lofty conception of the good and of happiness, and of the end or purpose of man, combined with his solid common sense and freedom from exaggeration, we may draw some strengthening comfort. Happiness to him consists in fulfilling man's true end, and this end is the unimpeded exercise of the highest powers or faculties of his soul in accordance with their proper virtues or excellences. Man's good is a certain life, and this life is a rational activity of the soul. That rational activity consists in moral action and in philosophic thought. Only in such rational activity is happiness found. Nevertheless it is not true that happiness is wholly independent of bodily or external goods, for with that curious aristocratic limitation characteristic of him, Aristotle holds that it is difficult for a person to do what is noble unless he is furnished with adequate external means. How far, then, can a man be happy who meets with much adversity and misfortune? Aristotle seeks to avoid exaggeration or paradox. Full happiness needs complete virtue and a complete life. It depends mainly upon the soul, its character, and its activities, but it also depends partly upon what befalls the soul. "For there are all sorts of changes and chances in life, and it is possible that the most prosperous of men will in his old age fall into extreme calamities, like Priam. But if a person has experienced such chances and has died a miserable death, nobody calls him happy."[90] Yet even to this exception there are limitations. Happiness depends essentially upon habitual activities of the soul, or, as we should add, upon character; and there is therefore something about it which is permanent, and is little liable to change. Hence it is not necessary or right to follow the changes of fortune, as if a man, with frequent alternation, were now happy and now miserable. True good and evil do not depend upon these changes, for though gifts of fortune are required as accessories, yet it is the excellent employment of his powers, and his activities in accordance with virtue, that constitute man's happiness, just as the reverse constitutes his misery. For nothing human is so permanent as the excellent exercise of our powers. Thus the truly happy man, who is always doing noble deeds or thinking lofty thoughts, will be just the one to bear the chances of life most nobly. And even in sore misfortunes—though the harm of them

may be that they may impede the finest exercise of the human powers—yet even in them beauty of character shines out, in the calm endurance of many great calamities, not through insensibility, but through nobility and greatness of soul. " And if it is the activities—what a man does—that determine the character of his life, then no happy man will become miserable, for he wi'l never do what is hateful and base. For we hold that the truly good and wise man will bear with seemliness whatever fortune sends, and will always do what is noblest in the circumstances." Finally, Aristotle makes a verbal, but important distinction. " If what we have said be true, the happy man can never become miserable or wretched, though he will not be blissful, if he meets with the fortunes of Priam."[91] " Blissful " is a poor translation of the Greek *makarios* : it means that kind of pure or superlative happiness which is, perhaps, best expressed in modern speech by the German words *selig* and *Seligkeit*.

It seems to me that there is something in Aristotle's simple, yet measured language and in his lofty thoughts which can give us comfort and fortitude even to-day.

One more word may be said of him before we pass on. Few of us can be philosophers, or can appreciate him when he speaks of the rapture and bliss of philosophic contemplation : the life of pure thought. Yet we too can agree that it is well " to make every effort to live in the exercise of the highest of our faculties," and that our reason is that part of us which is akin to the divine. And to some persons the interest of life and the exercise of intelligence *do* provide some comforts for the sorrows of life and its pains. We would prefer to be unhappy men than happy sparrows. " Who would lose, though full of pain, this intellectual being, those thoughts that wander through eternity?" So we should agree that there is a certain consolation in aiming at the highest, so far as in us lies,—" Zum höchsten Dasein immerfort zu streben."[92]

One other partly intellectual, partly aesthetic and partly moral, consolation was also felt by the Greek teachers—the contemplation of nature. Thus Plutarch says that " the world is a most holy and divine temple, into which man is introduced at his birth, not to behold motionless images made by hands, but those things (to use the language of Plato) which the divine mind has exhibited as the visible representations of the invisible, having innate in them the principle of life and motion, as the sun and the moon and the stars, and rivers ever growing with fresh water, and the earth affording sustenance to plants and animals. As life is an initiation into these things, it should be full of content and of joy." Some verses attributed to Aesop declare that " in the beauties of nature—earth and sea, stars, sun and moon—lie all the pleasure of man; the rest is only fears and pains." And Anaxagoras, when asked why one should choose to be born rather than not, replied, " for the sake of viewing the heavens and the whole order of the universe." This thought was, as we shall see, adopted and given a peculiar significance by the Stoics."³

In the first century of our era, philosophy was prevailingly ethical and practical. The philosopher who, as regards systems, was sometimes an eclectic, often became a sort of practical guide in life's affairs, and still more a sort of spiritual director. His rôle was to exhort, to fortify, to comfort; he fulfilled some of the tasks of a clergyman of to-day. Letters of consolation were written to those who had suffered bereavements, and these letters, which were really essays, were sometimes subsequently published. From Plutarch, who, in philosophy, cultivated a gentle eclecticism, we have two such letters, one to his wife on the death of their little daughter (Plutarch being away from home), and one to a friend on the death of his son. It is interesting to observe how far the commonplaces of consolation have changed, and how far they have remained the same, throughout the ages.

To his wife Plutarch, first of all, urges the blessings of memory. The two years of happiness which the dear child gave them were brief, but the joy was not less real and sweet because it was short. We ought not to forget past happiness because of present sorrow. So elsewhere he says that we must seek to mix together good and evil in our thought, and to rub out, or make dim, the evil by the good. We cannot expect to meet with no griefs; so we must take the good with the bad, and make the mixture of life seemly and harmonious. As for the child, he says, " what evil can we mourn for on her account if her pains are over? She did not, it is true, enjoy the pleasures of womanhood : but she cannot be said to have been deprived of them, for how can one be deprived of what one has never experienced?" Then he touches upon immortality, and speaks of it with more confidence to his wife than he does to his friend; he and she have both been initiated into the mysteries of Dionysus. The soul he regards as pre-existent: and " that soul which was but a short time in a human body, which sojourned only a brief space in this dark and mortal life, more quickly recovers the light and blaze of its former bright existence."

To his friend Appollonius he is somewhat more conventional. He recalls to him the universality of death: sooner or later it comes to all. Death is the end of all pain and sorrow: if it is an endless sleep, what is there evil in it? And if death be absolute annihilation, if, as Epicharmus says, what was united is now dissolved, if earth returns to earth, and the spirit to realms above, what in all this is grievous? In view of life's numerous sorrows many hold that not to be born is best, and, next, to die soon. " That your son died young may mean perchance that he was taken away from evils to come: whom the gods love die young. Remember how, when Xenophon, as he was sacrificing, was told that his son had died upon the battle field, he pulled the garland from his head, and asked how he fell; and when it was told him that his son died gallantly, after pausing to collect his thoughts, and quiet his emotion, he replaced the garland, and said, I did not ask the gods that my son should be long lived, for I could not know that this would be best for him, but I prayed that he might be good and a lover of his country, and I have my desire. Xenophon was right, for not length of life is important, but nobility, and even sudden death makes no real difference. The inevitable should not be regarded as hard. Life and all things in it are only lent to us by the gods: we should return their loans without a murmur. It was against nature, you say. He should have buried me, not I him. It was against our *human* nature, as we reckon things, but perhaps not against the providence of the whole or the order of the universe. For your son had attained to blissfulness; there was no need that he should tarry longer here. And if the sayings of the philosophers are true, as there is probability to think, then your son has past from mortal life to eternity, and lives in happiness among the blest."[4]

Thus does Plutarch console his friend, adding many a story and many a quotation from the poets. In his consolations there is an odd mixture of thoughts which we still use (though not always in the way in which he puts them), and of thoughts that have now become obsolete or empty: perhaps, too, there are ideas or touches which we can add to our own store.

Among all Greek writings which have been preserved to us, the largest material for the subject of the present essay is undoubtedly to be found in the literature of the Stoics, and more especially in those two latter day Stoics, Epictetus and Marcus Aurelius. To them might be added the writings of Seneca, though, in order not to make this essay unduly long, and as the language in which Seneca wrote was Latin, though his thought is mainly Greek, I shall in my quotations confine myself almost exclusively to the Emperor and the Slave.

There are some special reasons why the Stoics are of interest and value to us for our present subject, dealing, as it does, with the ethical and religious questions that concern the human heart, and seeking to bring together the contributions of the Hebrew and the Greek.

Zeno, the founder of Stoicism, was born in Cyprus, and was apparently a Phœnician. The dates of his birth and death are approximately 336-264 B.C. His two great immediate successors, Cleanthes and Chrysippus, both came from Asia Minor. Indeed " no single Stoic of note was a native of Greece proper." How far their eastern origin, and, for some of them, their Semitic blood, may have affected their teaching, and given to it some of its most characteristic features in ethics and religion, is a controverted question into which I cannot enter here. It has been strongly maintained, and no less strongly denied. But, at any rate, these are the facts. The three great formative Stoics of the first period, and the two great teachers of the middle period (Panaetius and Posidonius), were none of them born upon the Greek mainland. Only one—Panaetius—is as near it as Rhodes. The other four are all Orientals, for Cytium of Cyprus, Zeno's birthplace, was a colony of the Phœnicians. In them East and West meet together, and it is conceivable that the product is due in some measure to the confluence.[94a]

However all this may be, it is without question that Stoicism and Judaism present points of likeness as well as of contrast. Their likenesses are sufficient to make Stoic teaching in several matters complementary to Jewish teachings; we can add Stoic motives to Jewish motives for right doing; we can add Stoic comforts to Jewish comforts; and we can be the richer for doing so. The Stoic motives and the Jewish motives; the Stoic comforts and the Jewish comforts, are not antagonistic to each other. We may unite them together in a higher synthesis or harmony.

For, over and above the points in which Greek and Hebrew thought, in ethical and religious matters, are sympathetic and complementary to each other, the intense moral earnestness of the Stoics, their immense interest in the problems of good and evil, their close identification of " wisdom " with " goodness," their doctrine of Providence, are all points in which their teaching is sympathetic or congenial to the Jew.

Then again, that teaching happens to touch often upon our

own particular problem, partly through its very nature and
partly because of the circumstances of the time. This last point
is more especially true of the age of Epictetus and Aurelius.
For the Stoics were far from being mere philosophers of the
study and the lamp. They looked out upon humanity and its
troubles and its wounds. They were anxious to comfort, to
fortify, to heal. The office of spiritual doctor was in request :
they sought to discharge its duties. Amid the corruptions of
luxury and material civilization, on the one hand, amid the
uncertainties and vicissitudes of life, upon the other, they desired
to hold aloft the banner of simplicity, courage, and purity. A
Caligula, a Nero, a Domitian, might possess unlimited power
over the body : he might give free vent to his passions, his
cruelty, his avarice, his lust. The Stoics would show that he
need have no power over the soul : they would argue and prove
that knowledge and virtue, wisdom and righteousness, were still
realities, were still the higher and the more universal forces
and powers of the world, in accordance with its true nature as
well as with the true nature of man, and that it was still worth
while to pursue and to exhibit them. Indeed their teaching and
life should go to prove that nothing else was worth while at all.

It is difficult to give any account of Stoic " comforts " without a general statement of Stoic doctrine, and this would clearly
be quite impracticable; even if I had the knowledge and the
skill, there is here neither space nor opportunity.

Like many other teachers, the Stoics, and perhaps the three
great Stoics of the latest period more · especially (Seneca,
Epictetus, Aurelius), are full of contrasts and inconsistencies.
All is for the best; yet the world of men is full of evil. Man is
the highest of nature's works; yet there are few men who fulfil
the law of their being. And so on. Nevertheless, in spite of
inconsistencies, there is much which they say that still appeals
to us and will always appeal.

The ultimate basis of their comfort seems to us strangely
hollow and unsatisfactory. They were optimists of a curious kind.
" Whatever is, is right " was their doctrine, but it was set
forth according to a theory that seems to us oddly inadequate.
A Theist to-day might conceivably allow that " whatever is, is
right." In other words he might hold that there is a divine
purpose in all we call " evil," and that therefore it is always
being overruled for good, or transmuted into good, just as it
will finally be overcome and consumed by good. But the Stoic
optimism was different. To them the universe as such is

perfect, for the universe, or, at least, its soul, its immanent ruling and rational principle, is God. If the whole is perfect, then the parts are perfect too. Are earthquakes and volcanos as good and necessary as harvest and fruit trees? They are,—from the point of view, and to the knowledge, of the whole. Was the " maker " of the lamb the " maker " of the tiger? Yes, all within the world is the world's product. A rational principle is in all things : the sovereign reason, which is equivalent to divine providence, which again is nearly equivalent (at least to the later Stoics) to what we mean by the " goodness of God," is as responsible for, and as much the author of, the volcano as the fruit tree, the tiger as the lamb. Stoic faith goes far and needs some effort ! Suppose we accept it, but raise the greater difficulty. If the world is perfect in all its parts, one part is man. As God sees things, is man perfect too? Is all he calls pain and sorrow and misery no evil? And, above all, are his wickedness and ignorance no evil? Here the Stoics make a distinction. Their doctrine, put in everyday and untechnical words of our own age, seems to come to this. To man alone has been given the knowledge of good and evil, and the power to do and to be evil as well as good. In him and in his actions there *is* evil, though his evil is, and will be, overborne by the whole world's good. He alone is able to do what is rational or irrational consciously and of his own deliberate will. He alone is, or can make himself, truly free. A lily always achieves its good, but unconsciously. Man can fail. Success or failure is within his own power. Just as he need not *suffer* evil, so also need he not *commit* it. The Stoics, indeed, do not formulate this doctrine of free power for good or evil, knowledge or ignorance, so sharply, but it seems to be implicit in their very summons to man to learn and choose the good. Nor is it really contradicted by their teaching that all sin is ignorance, and that almost all men are ignorant.

The " paradox "—and yet the " comfort "—of Stoicism is brought out in the reply to the next objection. " No man need commit evil " : such a statement may perhaps pass. But " no man need suffer evil " seems wholly absurd. No man, even as things are, need undergo pain and misery ! Are not the innocent every day suffering at the hands of the guilty? Need none fall victims to poverty or disease? What of the sorrows of separation and of death? Then the Stoic replies : " I did not say that man need not suffer poverty or disease or banishment or privation or the loss of friends and of children. What

I do say is that he need not suffer *evil !*" What? Are none of these things evil? " None. The only true good and the only true evil are in the will. The good will is the only true good; the bad will is the only true evil. Whatever is not in my own power, whatever comes to me from without, whatever depends upon another man, or upon an accident or incident of nature, is *for me* neither truly good nor truly evil. So far as I do harm to another, that is *for me* truly an evil; to the ' sufferer ' it is none." A paradox truly, and yet a paradox which could fortify noble souls to noble deeds and noble endurance. Good and evil are placed *within* the soul : what is not mine, and does not issue from me, cannot make me better or worse. My well-being depends upon *me* and upon what *I* do : never upon what *you* do to *me.* Hence my well-being may be complete, when I suffer what the world calls terrible evils : and my ill-being may be complete, when I enjoy what the world calls the greatest goods. What is my true self? Not my body; but my soul, my reason, my ruling principle, my kinship with God. And this soul, or ruling principle of mine, has the power to make any event or sensation or impression a true evil or not. My soul can be evilly affected by such event, sensation or impression, or not. It can triumph over them, and be undisturbed, or it can yield. All depends upon the judgment which I make as to these events, sensations, impressions, whether I assess them truly or not—whether I realise their externality. Moreover, in addition to my reason, I have desires, impulses, passions and aversions. The reason by false judgment can become the servant of these desires and passions, and it is then injured in its nature and in its working. The will then produces a wrong act based upon a false judgment. It does and it suffers evil. Then our true end or purpose is not fulfilled : we act in accordance neither with our own true nature nor with the nature of the universe or of God. Well-being, then, consists in fulfilling the end of man, in acting according to his true nature. And this true nature is expressed in social acts and in moral and intellectual virtues—in justice, and kindness, and courage, and self-control, and truth, and so on throughout the list. Well-being, or happiness, is not pleasure or any kind of feeling : it is the free, unclouded exercise of the will; it is the will as formed and perfected by such constant, free and unclouded exercise. It is serenity and peace of soul, unsullied by passions and desires, always able to see all things (whether what the world calls good or what the world calls evil, whether they befall the self or another) as they truly and absolutely are.

It is not difficult to criticize such a doctrine, and to put one's finger upon its weaknesses and its gaps. One can explain its misconception of the place and function of the feelings; its false identification of ignorance and wickedness, of virtue and knowledge; one can dwell upon its crude, materialistic pantheism; its hopeless inadequacy when confronted with the awful problems of evil; its odd inconsistencies and paradoxes. But it nevertheless remains a notable achievement, and one which had great effects for good. It left its mark, and we are to-day the better because of Stoicism. We are the better for it unconsciously, for it has entered, though we may be unaware of it, into the texture of our common thought. But we can also become the better for it consciously. As we read its literature, we can be braced by its pure and lofty air.

Let us, then, now hear an enunciation of such Stoic doctrine as is relative to our special subject in the words of Epictetus and Aurelius themselves—of the Slave who (as men count possessions) possessed nothing, of the Emperor who possessed all. Let us start with the doctrine that no evil can befall a man unless he choose. For the only true evil, as the only true good, lie within—in the condition of the soul, the reason, the will. Not externals, but our judgment or opinion of externals, is what causes fear, perturbation, sorrow, unhappiness, and dims and corrupts the soul. The external is not our own, and it includes all our supposed " possessions "—friends, children, wife, property, and even our bodies. Whatever happens to these,—pleasure, pain, loss, death,—is also external, and is never for us a good or an evil. " Seek not the good," says Epictetus, " in external things ; seek it in yourself, or you will not find it."[95] " Where is the good? In the will. Where lies evil? In the will. Where is the neutral sphere? In the region outside the will's control." But " what do we admire? External things. What are we anxious about? External things. And yet we are at a loss to know why fear or anxiety assail us ! What else can possibly happen when we count impending events as evil? We cannot be free from fear, we cannot be free from anxiety. Yet we say, O Lord God, how am I to be rid of anxiety? Has He not given you endurance, has He not given you greatness of mind, has He not given you manliness? "[96] Only in respect of what I fear can any tyrant threaten me. For then, " who is there left for me to fear, and over what has he control? Over what is in my power? No one controls that. Over what is not in my power (e.g., the body).

I have no concern in that."[97] A man complains of an evil, but it is not the occurrence, the thing which befalls him, that is evil, but only his opinion about it which he adds to it. "My father gives me nothing. True; but to say that this is an evil is something which must be added to the fact, and falsely added. Therefore it is not poverty that we must cast out, but our judgment about poverty, and then we shall be at peace."[98]

Marcus Aurelius, the Emperor, in his secret self-communings, which a strange accident has preserved for the wonder and delight of all subsequent ages, impresses upon himself the same austere doctrine. "That which does not make a man himself worse cannot make his life worse either, nor injure it, whether from without or within."[99] "Efface the opinion, I am harmed, and at once the feeling of being harmed disappears: efface the feeling, and the harm disappears at once."[100] "If I do not consider what has befallen me to be an evil, I am unhurt. And I can refuse so to consider it."[101] "This day I have got rid of all trouble; or rather I have cast out all trouble, for it was not from without, but within, in my own imagination" (or opinion, or impression).[102] "The mind, unmastered by passions, is a very citadel, for a man has no fortress more impregnable, wherein to find refuge and be untaken for ever."[103] "Be like a headland of rock on which the waves break incessantly: but it stands fast, and around it the seething of the waters sinks to rest. 'Ah, unfortunate am I that this has befallen me.' Say not so. Does what has befallen you hinder you one whit from being just, high-minded, self-controlled, modest, free,—from possessing the qualities the presence of which enables a man's nature to come fully into its own? So if ought painful befall you, use this judgment: This is no misfortune, but to bear it nobly is good fortune."[104]

The doctrine is pushed by Epictetus to the utmost extremity. The loss of friend or son is put on the same level as the loss of property. It is outside the will, and not an evil. How we react to it—whether complainingly or bravely—here is the evil or the good. "Never say about anything, I have lost it, but say, I have restored it. Is your son dead? He has been restored. Is your wife dead? She has been restored."[105] "It is not that which happens which afflicts a man, for it does not afflict another, but it is his opinion about it which afflicts him."[106] The commonplace that all men are mortal is elevated into a tremendous doctrine of endurance. "He whom you love is mortal, and that which you love is not your own; it is not given you for ever. If you wish for son or friend, when it is not given you to have him, you are longing for a fig in winter."[107] " We ought not to let anyone make us miserable, but to let every-one make us happy, and God above all, who created us for this."[108] " How can a man be good who knows not who he is, and how can he know this when he has forgotten that all things that have come into being are perishable, and that it is impossible for man to be with man for ever? Now to desire what is impossible is slavish and silly : it is to make oneself a stranger in the world, and to fight against God with one's own judgments, as alone one can."[109] The wise man sits loose to all externals, including his body. " Purify your judgments, and see that nothing that is not your own is attached to you or clings to you, that nothing shall give you pain if it is torn from you."[110] " For the good man nothing is evil, whether he lives or dies."[111] On the other hand, do an evil deed, respond falsely to an impression, an event, and at once you suffer evil. The reward of evil is in itself, and the reward of goodness is in itself. " Do you seek a reward for a good man greater than doing what is good and just? " (So Seneca. " Do you ask what I seek from virtue? I answer, Itself. Virtue is its own reward. *Ipsa pretium sui* ").[112] " Never does a man do wrong in one thing, and suffer in another." " No man can do what is unjust without paying for it."[113]

Epictetus goes the length of denying that we ought to feel any more grief for the false " afflictions " of another than we do for our own. It is not that he preaches a self-centred isolation. Man is essentially social. He can only realise himself, and fulfil his own nature, by serving and helping others. But to grieve for another's loss would not only cloud the serenity of your soul—it would not only by the very fact of your grief be an accusation against God—but it would also be an acknowledgment that the loss to that other was of more than an external. Hence, whether for your own earache, or for another's loss, you must not lament internally, you must not, " groan from your inner being."[114] To do so would show a lack of faith in the world's order and in God.

It is clear that a determined detachment of this kind to all the incidents and calamities of life is at the same time a gigantic vindication of God. If there *is* no evil, except what you bring upon yourself by your own folly and passion and sin, then the whole awful question falls. It falls all the more completely if another's sin can never cause you evil. Then God is truly guilt-less. And this is the view which Epictetus takes. He makes

God say : " Come and bear witness for me. Is anything good or
evil which lies outside the range of the will? Do I harm anyone?
Do I put each man's advantage elsewhere than in himself?"[115]
Therefore Epictetus is always impressing upon us the duty of
accepting whatever befalls us as the will of God—of the Mind of
the perfect whole—and accepting it cheerfully, unrepiningly.
"For my part," he says, " I would wish death to overtake me
occupied with nothing but the care of my will, trying to make it
calm, unhindered, unconstrained, free. I would fain be found
so employed that I may say to God, Did I transgress thy commands? Did I ever accuse thee? Did I ever find fault with thine
administration? I fell sick when it was thy will, but I rebelled
not. I became poor when thou didst will it, but I rejoiced in my
poverty. I held no office, because it was thy will : I never coveted
office. Didst thou ever see me gloomy for that reason? Did I
ever come before thee but with a cheerful face, ready for any
commands or orders that thou mightest give? Now it is thy will
for me to leave the festival. I go, giving all thanks to thee, that
thou didst deign to let me share thy festival, and see thy works,
and understand thy government."[116] The strength, the stimulus,
the elevation of such a passage—who can deny it? We must
make the utmost effort for peace and freedom. " Lift up your
head at last, as one released from slavery. Dare to look up to
God and say, Deal with me hereafter as thou wilt, I am as one
with thee, I am thine. I flinch from nothing so long as thou
thinkest it good. Lead me whither thou wilt. Wouldst thou
have me hold office or eschew it, stay here or be an exile, be poor
or rich? For all this I will defend thee before men. I will show
each thing in its true nature, as it is."[117] And Epictetus argues
that it is only by this religious relation to God (of whom he asks
so little !) that this peace of mind, this ready acceptance of
destiny, can be attained. We cannot, it may well be, imitate
Hercules or Theseus. We cannot go about the world, clearing it
of wrong and lawlessness. We can, however, seek to cleanse our
own heart, " to cast out from our minds pain, fear, desire, ill
will, avarice, cowardice, passion uncontrolled. Yet these things
we cannot cast out unless we look to God alone, on Him set our
thoughts, and consecrate ourselves to His commands. If we wish
for anything else, with groaning and sorrow we shall have to
follow what is stronger than we, ever seeking peace outside ourselves, and never able to be at peace : for we seek it where it is
not, and refuse to seek it where it is."[118] The lofty spirits of
Judaism and Stoicism meet together in thought and are at one.

" The Lord gave: the Lord has taken away: blessed be the name of the Lord." So essentially Epictetus, even though his God is less " personal " than Job's. One must attach oneself to God. What does attach oneself mean? " That what God wills, we shall will too, and what He wills not, we too shall not will."[119] And this satisfied resignation to the order of events in our lives, we are to attain by examining the purposes of God and His governance of the world. " What has He given me to be my own and independent, what has He reserved for Himself? He has given me all that lies within the sphere of my choice, and has put it in my hands, unfettered, unhindered. How could He make my clay body free from hindrance? My property, my chattels, my honour, my children, my wife, He made subject to the revolution of the universe. Why then do I fight against God? Why do I will what is not for me to will, what is not given to me to hold under all conditions, but to hold only as it is given and so far as it is given? Suppose that He that gave takes away. Why then do I resist? I shall not merely be silly, if I try to compel Him that is stronger; first of all I shall be doing wrong. For whence did I bring what I have into the world? My father gave them me. And who gave them him? Who is it that made the sun, and the fruits of the earth, and the seasons, and the union and fellowship of men with one another? You have received everything, nay your very self, from Another, and yet you complain and blame the Giver, if He takes anything away from you?* Who are you and for what have you come? Did not He bring you into the world? Did not He show you the light? Has He not given you senses too and reason? And in what character did He bring you into life? Was it not as a mortal, one who should live upon earth with his little portion of flesh, and behold God's governance, and share for a little while in His pageant and His festival? Will you not then look at the pageant and the festal gathering as long as it is given you, and then, when God leads you forth, go away with an obeisance to Him and thanksgiving for what you have heard and seen?"[120] Epictetus has a keen eye and spirit for the wonders of nature: the great primal elements and the heavenly bodies, to him no less divine than man, were a comfort to him in themselves. " When a man has such things to think on, and sees the sun, the moon and stars,

---

* The " Loan " argument is also common. Our " property " is lent to us. We must restore it when called upon without a murmur. " The most detestable kind of debtor," says Seneca, " is he who rails at his creditor."

and enjoys earth and sea, he is not forlorn, he is not alone." Or if alone, yet if he knows what is his own, and what is alien to him, or lent to him, he has within him a great peace, the peace proclaimed not by the Emperor, but, through the voice of reason, by God. He possesses the true, the unassailable liberty.[121]

Aurelius, like Epictetus, preaches the same resignation to the divine will; he is full of the same assurance that " external evils " are in no wise to be regarded as to the discredit of God. The gods put it wholly in man's power not to fall into evils that are truly such. " The Nature of the Whole (i.e., God) would not have shown such powerlessness or unskilfulness as to allow good and evil to fall without any discrimination alike upon the evil and the good. But death and life, honour and dishonour, pain and pleasure, riches and poverty, do equally befall the good and the bad. Therefore they are neither good nor evil." " Nothing can happen to a man which is not a contingency natural to man. If then only the natural and usual befall you, why be angry? The Common Nature (i.e., God) brings you nothing which you cannot bear."[122] " All must submit: the pig screams when it is sacrificed: to man, the rational creature, it has alone been granted to submit willingly to all that happens."[123] " All that is in tune with thee, O Universe, is in tune with me. Nothing that is in due time for thee is too early or too late for me. All that thy seasons bring, O Nature, is fruit for me. All things come from thee, subsist in thee, go back to thee. The poet says, Dear city of Cecrops. Will you not say, Dear City of Zeus?"[124] In addition to this sheer resignation, Aurelius seems to believe that there is some kind of divine co-operation with man in the things which are within his power. " Begin at any rate with prayers for such things, and you will see. Instead of praying, How may I be quit of that man?, pray, How may I not wish to be quit of him? Not, May I not lose my little child, but, How may I not fear to lose him? Give your prayers this turn, and see what comes of it."[125] Yet, in spite of this more Theistic touch, Aurelius is more weary of life than Epictetus: it is a greater effort to the burdened Emperor to keep upon the heights of cheerful resignation: he is more inclined to see vanity and sameness and insignificance and transitoriness, and to be oppressed by what he sees. Still he struggles to keep his Stoic faith. " How tiny a fragment of the boundless abyss of time has been appointed to each man. For in a moment it is lost in eternity. And how tiny a part of the universal substance, and of the Universal Soul! On how tiny a clod of the whole earth do you crawl. Keeping

all these things in mind, think nothing of moment save to do
what your nature leads you to do, and to bear what the Universal
Nature brings you."[126] The universe itself is ever fair and
young and in its prime. It is all opinion, he reminds himself
again and again. Make that right, and there need be no trouble
or tempest, but a great calm and a waveless sea.

For the most part Epictetus has no explanation or palliative
of the ordinary calamities and afflictions of man to offer beyond
the sheer denial that they are or can be evil. They are external
to the will: therefore they are not evil. They happen (so far as
they are not due to human folly or sin) in the course of nature
(e.g., disease): therefore they cannot be evil. Occasionally he
suggests that they are disciplines or opportunities—an old point
of view much emphasized by Seneca. If a man is poor, ill, exiled,
emprisoned, he should say, God sends these events to me, not
because he hates me, but he does it " for the purpose of exer-
cising me and making use of me as a witness to others." (So
Seneca. " Quare quaedam dura (boni) patiuntur? Ut alios pati
doceant. Nati sunt in exemplar.")[127] In this way we must use
the actions of bad men for our own profit. " He is a bad neighbour, you say. Yes, for himself; but he is good for me; he trains
me to be considerate and fair-minded."[128] So with illness, death,
insult and any other supposed " evil "; all can be made profit-
able. All can be made a means of blessedness and well-being.
As each trial comes, one should say, I was practising for *this*, I
was training for *this*. Fever, hunger, thirst, are God's questions:
have you kept the rules of training? They can be your proofs
that you have kept them. Are you a student of philosophy? To
what purpose except as a preparation for right living and for
obtaining happiness and tranquility?[129] If you bear your fever
aright, you have done your part as a sick man. "What does
bearing fever rightly mean? It means not to blame God or man,
not to be crushed by what happens, to await death in a right
spirit, to do what you are bid. This is what the moment requires
from the man in a fever: if he fulfils these requirements, he has
what is his own."[130] (In other words, " he has his reward.").
Seneca develops this idea with zest. " God does not pet the good
man: he tries him, hardens him and fits him for Himself. Let
him, He says, be exercised by labour, sufferings and losses, so
that he may gather true strength. Why does God afflict the best
of men with ill health, or sorrow, or other troubles? Because in
the army the most hazardous services are assigned to the bravest
soldiers. God hardens, reviews and exercises those whom He
tests and loves."[131]

The general Stoic theodicy or vindication of God was little
more than mere assertion. The universe was perfect, and each
part was necessary for the whole. It moved forward to its pre-
destined goal. That goal was of the most cheerless kind, and it
is strange that the human soul could find comfort in so curious
a doctrine. The world soul—materially conceived as subtlest
fire, and yet spiritually as purest reason—produced the universe
out of itself. And ultimately the universe would again be
reabsorbed in the God, or Fiery Reason, which gave it birth.
Then the process would start afresh, and precisely the same
things, creatures, persons, events, would be produced all over
again. And so on for ever! We marvel how these repeating
cycles of existence, tending nowhither, could seem to many noble
souls adequate as an explanation of the riddle and as a stimulus
to high endeavour. We may, however, conjecture that the
greater and more frequent appeal was to the universe as it was,
to its order, its beauty, its regular movements, its majesty. The
world, as a Kosmos, revealed God, and was God. To follow its
order, to understand its working, to live in harmony with its
reason, this seemed to the Stoic to be compensation for, and to
transfigure, all the pain and sorrow which life might bring.
The famous hymn of Cleanthes seeks to give what explanation is
possible on Stoic lines to the problem of evil in a perfect universe.
"O thou most glorious, invoked by many a name, almighty
evermore, who didst found the world and guidest all by law,—
O Zeus, hail! for it is right that all mortals should address thee.
We are thine offspring, alone of mortal things that live and walk
the earth, moulded in the image of the All; therefore thee will
I hymn and sing thy might continually. . . . Without thee,
O Lord, no deed is done on earth, nor in the ethereal vault
divine, nor in the deep, save only what wicked men do in the
folly of their hearts. Nay, what is uneven thy skill makes even;
thou bringest order out of disorder: and things not friendly are
friendly to thee. For thou hast fitted all things together, the good
with the evil, that there might be one eternal law over all."
And in another hymn he said, "Lead me, O Zeus, and lead me,
Destiny, the way that I am bid by you to go. To follow I am
ready. If I do not choose, I make myself wicked, and must
follow none the less."[132] These words were frequently in the
mouth of Epictetus. He too believed that even the bad cannot
in the long run hinder the working out of the divine drama. But
the right and glorious thing to do is to follow willingly and with
intelligence. Again, in such a composite universe, there must

be events like death or disease. We must take what comes, and deal with it as is fitting. Aurelius discusses the subject more frequently. In the privacy of his diary he even ventures to suggest the alternative that there may be no Providence, no Order: only a Welter of Confusion or Chance. Yet even so, surely to be good and rational is the better choice for man. " We are fellow workers," he says, " towards the fulfilment of one object, some of us knowingly and intelligently, others blindly."[133] Even the bad are needful. " One is a co-agent in this, another in that, and even he that murmurs and seeks to hinder or disannul what occurs. For the universe had need of such men also."[134] " As to the whole, if God—all is well: if haphazard—be not you also haphazard."[135] " All things come from that one source, from that ruling reason of the universe, either under a primary impulse from it or by way of consequence. And, therefore, the gape of the lion's jaws and poison and all noxious things, such as thorns and mud, are but after-results of the grand and the beautiful. Look not, then, on these as alien to that which you reverence, but turn your thoughts to the one source of all things."[136] The belief that there *is* a world order, that reason is at the heart of things, comforts the Emperor in spite of the vanities and burdens and tedium of his own solitary life. " If there be a unity, a plan, a providence, I bow in reverence, my feet are firmly planted, I put my trust in the power that rules."[137] He is convinced that all pain to the part must bring welfare to the whole. He even ventures to think that it must be of value to the welfare and perfection of God himself. There need be no worry about the so-called " miseries of the righteous," and the prosperity of the wicked, if we would only remember that pleasure is not a good and pain is not an evil. It is, indeed, impious to suppose so, for then we must inevitably find fault with God. If we judge that good and evil are the things in our power and these only, then we shall neither accuse God nor hate man.

Here we touch upon the Stoic consolations for the presence of evil, so far as it comes from the wickedness of man. They are curiously unlike the consolations of the Psalmists or the Rabbis. We hear nothing of the retribution of the wicked, whether in this world or in another; nothing of their destruction or disappearance or conversion, as the world " progresses " or draws nearer to the golden age. The world does not progress; the wicked do not cease; in the Psalmists' sense they are not punished. The Stoic consolations are different. The wicked only harm themselves; they cannot hurt the good. They sin by ignorance. They are, in some odd way, not antagonistic, perhaps they are even necessary, to the completeness and welfare of the Perfect Whole. Convert them, teach them, if you can: for the rest, bear with them, help them, even love them.

To begin with, then, there must be wicked, ignorant, boorish men. Why is never clearly explained, but the necessity is emphasized. "When you are offended at shamelessness in any one," muses the Emperor, "put this question to yourself: Can it be that shameless men should not exist in the world? It cannot be. Then ask not for what cannot be. As bad men must be, they must clearly act according to their ' badness.' To expect otherwise were madness."[138] Taken collectively, wickedness does no harm to the universe. It is obvious that if the universe is perfect, this must be so. And we saw that Cleanthes in his hymn declares that all men must somehow subserve the reason and purpose of the whole, whether willingly or unwillingly, whether sooner or later. This disposes of wickedness, so far as the universe is concerned: so far as man's fellow men are concerned, the wickedness of one does no harm to the other. It is harmful only to the doer. This hard saying depends upon the fundamental dogma that our wills are wholly ours, and that no outside thing or outside person can (if we so choose) injure or soil them. And in our wills lies the only true good or the only true evil. Hence the equal emphasis upon the social nature of man and upon the absolute independence of the individual. Aurelius puts the point with extraordinary clearness. " To my will the will of my neighbour is as indifferent (or purely neutral) as his vital breath and his flesh. For however much we are made for one another, yet our will has in each case its own sovereignty. For otherwise my neighbour's wickedness would be my evil: and this was not God's will, so that my misfortune should not be within the power of another."[139] He that does wrong, does wrong to himself. The unjust man is unjust to himself, for he makes himself bad. His vice is his ignorance; he mistakes evil for good and good for evil; he cannot help himself and his actions are inevitable. " If you can," says Aurelius, " convert him: if not, remember that kindliness was given you for this very end. It is indeed man's peculiar quality to love even the stumblers, and this love follows (or can spring forth) as you remember that such men are your kinsmen, that soon both they and you will be dead, and above all that they cannot hurt you."[140] One can only pity ignorance and forgive it. Epictetus takes precisely the same line, though he expresses it rather more drastically, as is his wont. " Remember that it is not he who reviles you, or strikes you, who insults you, but it is your opinion about these things as being insulting."[141] No other person can harm you unless you choose.[142] The wrong doer is deceived in his opinions, and he suffers the penalty. The deceived cannot be one person and the sufferer another. "Whoso remembers this will not be angry with any man, or vexed; he will not revile anyone or blame him; he will not quarrel with any man or hate him."[143] As usual Epictetus does not shrink from the most bizarre conclusions. The multitude do not know what is good and evil: they go astray. "Ought we then to be angry with them or to pity them? Only show them their error, and you will see how they will desist from their faults. What, you say; ought not this robber and this adulterer to be put to death? Not so. Say rather: Should I destroy this man who is in error about the greatest matters? That would be inhuman: it would be like saying, Should I not kill this blind man? If the greatest harm that can befall one is the loss of what is greatest, and a right will is the greatest thing in everyone, is it not enough for him to lose this without incurring your anger besides? Pity him rather than hate him. Why, indeed, are we angry? Because we admire the material things of which they rob us. Cease to admire your clothes, and you are not angry with him who steals them: cease to admire your wife's beauty, and you cease to be angry with the adulterer. Know that the thief and the adulterer have no place among things that are your own, but only among things that are another's and beyond your power. If you let them alone, and count them as nothing, you have no one to be angry with any more. But as long as you admire these things, you must be angry with yourself rather than with them. You have fine clothes, your neighbour has none; you have a window, you wish to air them. He does not know what is the true good of man, but fancies, as you do too, that it is to have fine clothes. Is he not to come then and carry them off?"[144] The strange confusion between a man's clothes and his wife and her honour show the limits of Stoic philosophy. Of the true interconnection of man with man, of the true way in which the hurt of those we love is our own hurt and their welfare ours, the Stoics had no real conception. Or shall we say that, in order to obtain this impossible independence of each individual, they deliberately falsified the facts, and refused to admit the true nature of friendship and of love? Yet within their limits, the doctrines of independence, of the true good, and of the explanation of wickedness by ignorance, have all their value. They led on, anyway, not only to mere endurance, but to good will, and not only to good will, but to charity. The ideal hero of Epictetus must possess " this special refinement: he must be flogged like an ass, and when he is flogged, he must love those who flog him, as if he were the father of all and the brother of all."[145]

We have seen that the great Stoic consolation in adversity is the individual's lofty independence, the inwardness of his true good, the impossibility of taking it away from him, the impregnable fortress of his inviolate reason and will. Yet, at the same time, it is no less a consolation, or at all events a stimulus and a fortification, for each individual to know that he is, by that very rational nature of his, united to his fellow man and to God. We have already heard how kinsmen cannot be hated, and how all men are our kinsmen, not as partakers of the same blood, but as sharing in the common reason, as parts of the one great Deity, united by a common relationship. We are citizens of a single city, and that city is the world. We are cosmopolitans. This thought seems to exercise a soothing effect upon the Stoic mind. We are constituted for fellowship. To live for oneself in the highest sense of the word is to live for others. " Delight in this one thing," says Aurelius, " and take your rest therein—from social act to go on to social act, remembering God."[146] " That is agreeable to every man's interest which is agreeable to his own constitution and nature. But my nature is rational and civic; my city and country, as Antoninus, is Rome: as a man, the world. The things then that are of advantage to these communities, these, and no other, are good for me."[147] And if it fortifies and soothes to remember our cosmopolitanism, it fortifies and consoles still more to remember our kinship with God. For this is man's privilege and glory: this is his high peculiarity: this it is which gives him the assurance of blessedness, if only he opens his eyes and exerts his will. " Are not our souls bound up and in close touch with God," exclaims Epictetus, " as parts and particles of Him?" " You are never alone: God is within you."[148] As such a separate, self-conscious, self-determined portion of God, man must imitate Him. " If the divine is faithful, man must also be faithful; if free, man must also be free; if beneficent, man must also be beneficent; if magnanimous, man must also be magnanimous."[149] If man and God are akin, why should he not " call himself a citizen of the world, why not a son of God, and why should he be afraid of anything which happens among men? Is kinship with the Emperor enough to make us live in safety and without fear? And to have God for our maker and father and guardian, shall this not release us from sorrows and fears?"[150] " If a man could only take to heart this judgment, as he ought, that we are all, before anything else, children of God, and that God is the Father of gods and of men, I think that he would never harbour a mean or ignoble thought about himself. Why, if the Emperor adopts you, your arrogance will be past all bearing; but if you realise that you are a son of Zeus, will you feel no elation ?"[151]

People have spoken of Stoic pride. But one cannot rightly say that either of the last two great Stoic teachers show anything of it. Independence, in the sense they give to it, is certainly not pride. Nor it is arrogance. It is true that both Epictetus and Aurelius are conscious that they are different from most men in aims and character, but it cannot be said that this truthful consciousness of a simple fact made them proud. It is another question how far it made them happy. There is a considerable difference in this respect between Epictetus and Aurelius. The poor freedman is far happier than the all powerful Emperor. His life was, after all, far less burdened with anxiety, responsibility and care; far less filled with sorrows, failures, disappointments. In spite of his poverty and his lameness, it was easier for him than for Aurelius to wear that cheerful face, to show that bright content, to feel that undimmed happiness, which should be the characteristic of the philosopher, and indeed of every man who knows the nature of good and evil and the secret of well-being. Nevertheless, though far more marked in Aurelius (as in Seneca), we find in Epictetus too, to some extent, the same curious contrast. On the one hand, there is the immense reverence for the universal order; the firm conviction that all is well, that the universe is natural and directed by a divine reason, which is also beneficent and even loving. On the other hand, there is the vivid sense of the transitoriness of all human affairs and endeavours, of the eternal sameness of things, and of the pettiness, the ignorance and squalor of far the larger portion of mankind. That the world would gradually become much better than it was, that mankind would grow less foolish and ignorant, that the quantity of true human good would therefore increase and the evil diminish—of all this there is no trace. In Epictetus, however, this contrast is only in so far implied that there is no indication of its opposite. No word is said to make us believe that the teacher was hopeful about the future of mankind or about the possibilities of average human character. No interest is displayed in the betterment of society as society, or of its institutions and organisation, as opposed to the betterment of the individual soul. In Aurelius the contrast is extremely poignant. His book is no lecture or discourse or essay. The Stoic is in undress. And as his passion for righteousness is, on this account, the more ennobling, his sadness becomes also the more piteous. There is no word about the marvel of Rome and the Empire, no worry or wonder how far the onset of the barbarians (and yet how valiantly he fought them!) could be stayed, no hope for the maintenance and development of Roman law, literature, civilisation. Beyond grand and austere injunctions to right doing and well-being, beyond reflections upon God and His relation to the universe and to man, we meet with little but sad confessions about the vanity of life and its terrible sameness and tedium. The majority of men are ignorant or vicious. What has been will recur. Soon— happily, soon—comes death, and with death forgetfulness and oblivion. Fame is idle and fleeting. The great and the small will be alike forgotten. So will one generation succeed another, till at the last this, our cycle, shall have an end, and a fresh cycle will begin, repeating the old events, the old follies, the old madnesses. It is strange, indeed, that so cheerless a world, so hopeless an outlook, should yet have seemed to prove, or to cohere with, a supreme Reason, a divine Intellect, a perfect Providence. It is needless to quote any of these mournful passages: our object is to display the consolations of Stoicism, not its regrets, its complaints, its disappointments. Only in one thing let us note the falsity of the great Emperor's expectation. His fame endures. We shall never forget him. But just as to a modern moralist to-day, who, in the presence of evil and oppressed by it, might argue that, even so, the only things worth living for are love and righteousness and beauty and knowledge, so was it with Aurelius. Though life is transitory, vain, full of tedium, live out the rational life, fulfil your true nature. After all, reason and well doing are somehow worth while. Amid the universal vanity, they, after all, are not vain. "But a little while, and you will be burnt ashes and a few dry bones, and possibly a name, or not even a name. And a name is but sound and a far-off echo. And all that men prize so highly in their lives is empty and rotten and paltry: they are as puppies snapping at each other, as quarrelsome children, now laughing and now in tears. What then remains? To wait with a good grace for the end, whether it be extinction or translation. Till then, what suffices? What but to reverence the gods and to praise them, to do good to men,

and to ' bear ' with them and ' forbear.' ''[152]   How tranquil,
how noble, how austere! Life passes; it is short; what is the
moral? Let us eat and drink, for to-morrow we die? No. "One
thing on earth is worth much—to live out our lives in truth and
justice, and in charity with liars and unjust men.''[153]   For
" this only is the harvest of earthly existence, a righteous disposition and social acts.''[154]   Life is a warfare and a pilgrim's
sojourn: the things of the body are as a river, and the things of
the soul (even these!) are vanity and as a dream, and posthumous
fame is forgetfulness. What is the one thing to help us on our
path? Philosophy . As if to-day we said: Religion. Again:
" fame is merely emptiness. Only one thing is worth our serious
zeal: a just mind, social acts, truthfulness and resignation to
all that befalls us.''[155]   To see things as they really are, to do
justly, and to speak the truth—that is life's salvation, " and the
only right and real enjoyment is to add good deed to good
deed, so as not to leave the smallest gap between.''[156]

Life was shorter in the Roman Empire than it is to-day. A
man of fifty thought himself already old. It was also more uncertain. To men in any prominence who lived under a Tiberius,
a Caligula, or a Nero, this uncertainty was immensely increased.
Even to a ruler like Aurelius the chance of death was never far
off. Moreover, apart from wars or the cruelties of wicked
emperors, a sadness hung over life. Yet many were afraid and
unwilling to die. The question whether death meant sheer
extinction or some other kind of existence was eagerly discussed.
Would such another life befall all men, or perchance only those
who had been initiated into some hidden mystery and redeemed
by some loftier knowledge? If earthly life became too intolerable, was it permitted, was it wise, to hasten the inevitable end
by one's own act? The Stoics did not seek to lead men's thoughts
away from death. They by no means agreed with Spinoza that
death was the last thing on which the wise man's time and
thoughts should be spent. ' Memento mori '; remember death:
make life its commentary: prepare for the end; these
were commonplaces acceptable to them and approved. And
the view they took of death was, on the whole, stern
and unyielding. Most of them held that the individual
soul ceased after death to have any further consciousness
or memory. In the ordinary sense of the word there
was no life beyond the grave. Yet from this grim
conclusion the Stoics drew no sad, no pessimistic moral. They
lodged no complaint against nature or God. They saw in such a

complete cessation of life no cause for fear or grumbling, no cause for slackness or frivolity. On the contrary. Death should be a lever for the finest and most strenuous life. There is something very elevated and sublime about this Stoic point of view, something too which affords us a certain austere and solemn consolaton, even though we do not share it, and even though we could not defend the arguments on which it rests. Death seemed to the Stoics a good and proper thing for two main reasons. Both were reasons which no one could possibly contradict or gainsay. In the first place, death was universal. It happened to all living things. Therefore it was obviously according to nature; nothing could well be more so! And if according to nature, it was according to God; it was a divine law; it was good. But, in the second place, death was even necessary for the universe. The death of its parts conditioned the life and continuance of the whole. The death of a plant, an animal, a man, means its resolution into the various elements of which it is composed. On the constant change of elements, on their never ceasing formation, dissolution and reformation, the life and progress of the whole depend. Changes preserve the universe: they keep it going! Thus, even theoretically, death is no evil, but a good . On the practical side, it was not difficult to argue that it was a universal refuge. Beyond its doors the tyrant could pursue his victim no further. As a mere negation or sleep, it was no object of terror. Looked at from the universal point of view it was a good. Regarded as outside the will, it was a matter of indifference. Kept ever before the mind, it should lead a man away from meanness and trivialities and wild desires to a strenuous and righteous life. It is clear that no *proof* that death should have this effect upon life is possible. The argument that because life is short and uncertain, the only sensible thing to do is to perform as many " good " and " social " actions as possible can only appeal to him who regards such actions as the best thing in life or as the most essential element in well being. A man, who regarded "pleasure" or sensuous enjoyments as the best thing, would draw the very opposite conclusion. Nevertheless, the fact remains—and it had its wide influence and effect—that, to the Stoic philosophy, death, in no wise an evil, seemed but a spur to the best and noblest life. It is thus that we find it reckoned both in Epictetus and Aurelius. " Death is not formidable, but only the fear of death." Sooner or later the dissolution which is death must take place. " Why ? That the revolution of the universe may be accomplished, for it has need of things present, things future, and things past and

done with."[157] Ears of corn are ripened that they may be reaped.
Just as naturally must men die. To pray that men should not
die would be like " a prayer not to be ripened, not to be reaped "
—not to fulfil the order of nature and the will of God. When
you die, " you will, indeed, no longer exist, but you will be
something else of which the world then will have need."[158]
Understand what death is, and there is nothing fearful about it,
nothing irrational. To Epictetus as to the Stoics generally, it is
not only a universal harbour of refuge, but it is the means open
to everybody, whereby, in the last resort, if it is absolutely impossible to live a man's true life, one may withdraw and give up
the game. It is the final reason why we need never despair or
complain of life. For if the conditions become intolerable, we
can bring them to an end. This is the famous Stoic doctrine of
suicide, or the " open door."[158a] However deeply we may
disagree with it, one must remember that the best of the Stoic
teachers only recommended it as a last resource, when the possibility of a " noble " life appeared hopeless, or as an anticipation
of a death already imminent by a tyrant's decree or an incurable
disease. Much more commonly it was right to await the order of
nature, which was the signal of God. " When He releases you
from this service, then shall you depart to Him : but for the present be content to dwell in this country wherein He appointed you
to dwell."[159] Aurelius takes practically the same line. But he
emphasizes more than Epictetus the driving force of death as a
stimulus to noble life. " Do every act of your life as if it were
your last." " Let your every deed and word and thought be
those of a man who can depart from life this moment." " Behave
not as though you had ten thousand years to live. Your doom
hangs over you; while you live, while you may, become good."[160]
He dwells repeatedly on the thought that no man can possess
either the past or the future. One has only the momentary present. Hence, at death, the longest and the shortest life part with
the same quantity of time. It is really, therefore, of no importance
whether one dies after many years or to-morrow. In comparison
with eternity human life is a mere moment. The life of a baby
of three days, the life of a Nestor of three centuries ,are as one.
Do not repine at the order of nature. The Emperor, like
Epictetus, considers that change and dissolution are necessary
for the world. " The changes not only of the elements, but of
the things compounded of them, preserve the Universe." " All
things must change, be transformed and perish, that other things
may in their turn come into being."[161] Death is only a function

of nature; and if a man be frightened by a function of nature, he
is childish; moreover, death is not only a function of nature, but
an advantage to nature. Therefore welcome it . The Emperor
muses as to the possibility of another life. While he leaves the
matter open, he tends upon the whole to reject it, and he is very
far from making his faith in a " world order " in any degree
depend upon it. The passage is highly curious and characteristic.
" How can the gods, after disposing of all things well and with
good will towards men, have overlooked this one thing that some
men, and they especially good men, who have had as it were the
closest commerce with the Divine, and by devout conduct and
acts of worship have been in the most intimate fellowship with
it, should, when once dead, have no second existence, but be
wholly extinguished? But if this indeed be so, know assuredly
that they would have ordained it otherwise, had it needed to be
otherwise. For had it been just, it would also have been feasible,
and had it been in conformity with Nature, Nature would have
brought it about. Therefore from its not being so, if indeed it is
not so, be assured that it ought not to have been so. For you
can see yourself that in this fruitless enquiry you are arguing
with God. But we should not thus reason with the gods, if they
were not perfectly good and just. But if they are, they would not
have overlooked anything being wrongly and irrationally
neglected in their thorough ordering of the Universe." In other
words, as the whole world is perfect and rational, whatever
happens to ourselves, a part of the world, must be for the best—
at least for the world![162]

In either case we must await the event with readiness and
calm. To the weary Emperor upon his throne—burdened with
ceaseless and unattractive toil, compelled to live among people
most of whom were unsympathetic to him—the prospect of
death was a comfort rather than a dread. There are few
passages of literature more intensely pathetic than the following words wrung from the inmost depths of this great and solitary soul. " If you desire a commonplace solace that will
appeal to your heart, nothing will enable you to meet death with
equanimity better than to observe the environment you are
leaving, and the sort of characters with whom your soul will no
longer be mixed up. For while it is very far from right to be
disgusted with them, but rather even to befriend and deal
gently with them, yet it is well to remember that not from men
of like principles with yours will your release be. For this
alone, if anything, could draw one back and bind one to life, if

it were but permitted to live with those who have possessed themselves of the same principles as one's own. But now you see how you are driven, by sheer weariness at the jarring discord of your life with them, to say : Tarry not, O death, lest peradventure I too forget myself."[143] The final conclusion is indicated with incomparable austerity and dignity at the end of his diary. What comes in its season must be well. To the wise and the just, it must be the same if their acts in obedience to right reason are few or many, and a matter of indifference whether they look upon the world for a longer or a shorter time. " Man, you have been a citizen in this world-city, what matters it to you, if for five years or a hundred ? For under its laws equal treatment is meted out to all. What hardship then is there in being banished from the city, not by a tyrant, or an unjust judge, but by Nature who introduced you into it ? So might a praetor, who commissions a comic actor, dismiss him from the stage. *But I have not played my five acts, but only three.* True, but in life three acts count as a full play. For He that is responsible for your composition originally and your dissolution now, decides when it is complete. You are responsible for neither. Depart then with a good grace, for He that dismisses you is gracious."[164]

It is no part of this essay to discuss or estimate the effects of Stoicism. Nor can I even say anything about the lives and the deaths of the men who were inspired by its teaching. The readers of Tacitus know that, at any rate, it helped men to die nobly at one of the worst epochs of Rome's long history. There are those who make a mock of Seneca, but it is easier to condemn him than to estimate him fairly. It may be questioned how far many of his critics could have withstood the immense difficulties of his situation and the peculiar subtlety of his temptations. Even if we surrender him to the wolves, Stoicism, from Zeno to Aurelius, can yet boast a number of useful and noble lives of whom we know, and it must have fashioned a far greater number of useful and noble lives whose names will be for ever unknown.

Nor will I attempt to lengthen a study that is already far too long by any general summary or appraisal. If I have dwelt longer upon, and quoted more fully from, the Greeks than the Hebrews, this is only because the words of the Hebrews are more familiar to my readers than the words of the Greeks. Our chief comforts and consolations spring from Jerusalem and not from Athens. Yet surely the collocation of the two " comforts," the

Hebrew and the Greek, is peculiarly interesting and valuable. The two together make a striking combination, a treasury from which each of us can draw according to our needs. Sometimes they run on different lines; sometimes they meet upon the heights (for there is a kinship in genius); they are often complementary to one another; rarely contradictory or opposed. So we may leave them. On their synthesis or reconciliation, their union and higher harmony, the reader may meditate for himself.

It may, however, be noted that for both Judaism and Stoicism (for I will not further take account of other phases of Hellenic thought) the ultimate comfort lies in the rationality of the universe. It is not a mere toss up. It has a meaning. And in the idea of rationality is included the idea of righteousness. There is, it is held, a kinship between them. If the world, or the soul of the world, is rational, it is also righteous, and makes for righteousness. The Stoic and the Jew interpret, or fill out, this fundamental faith, assertion, comfort, very differently, but the basis is the same. The world has a meaning and a rational meaning. If rational, righteous; if righteous, good. The world *is* good, says the Stoic; or, again, the soul, the rational principle, of the world is good. The world *is* good, and is governed by goodness, says the Jew. There is a difference between the two statements, but they approach, and sometimes even approximate to, each other.

What this rationality and goodness imply is another matter. To the one, they may imply world conflagrations, cyclic repetitions; to the other, the Golden or Messianic Age. To us, perhaps, neither the one nor quite the other. But more fundamental than the implications are the rationality, the goodness, in themselves.

Again, common to both Judaism and Stoicism is the faith that man possesses a peculiar kinship to the world-reason, the world-goodness. Man like the world is rational; like the world, he is, or rather he can become, "good." Moreover, in virtue of this kinship, there is commerce, there is relationship, between the derivative reason and its source. In this communion lies comfort. It is true that in Stoicism this communion is limited by its inadequate conception of the supreme Reason and (as it seems to me) of the "personality" of God. But in the kinship itself, and in the results of that kinship, both religions (for we may call Stoicism a religion) find strength and consolation.

Both, in the next place, are agreed that there is value in

life, value in man. What is that value? It is something inward.. It is the kinship between man and God. It is the human reason, or soul, with its appropriate functions and actions: thought and righteousness. In spite of all " external " evils, in spite of the far truer evil of sin (whereby the soul itself degrades and defiles itself), there is in life, there is in man, an absolute value. It is this comfort which, as we have seen, is so magnificently expressed by Stoicism. Come pain, come death, come what will, the Soul retains its absolute value, its sovereign worth, its supreme independence. Even if it were the only Soul, the only Reason, in the world, even if it endure but for a moment, and if when it passes, it is destroyed for ever, yet while it exists, it can never deny its own greatness, its own value. It will never give the lie unto itself. It holds itself erect and unconquerable even—if it were so, though it is not so—against a dumb and an alien world. Is not Judaism at one with Stoicism here? " For all is vanity *except that pure soul*, which must hereafter appear before the throne of thy glory."

We need not catalogue Stoic limitations and exaggerations, or mention the values which it has depreciated or denied. Do we hold to-day that all is *not* vanity except the soul? Or that the soul *causes* the not-soul to possess value? It is also undeniable that in the relation of soul with soul, just as in the relation of the human soul with the world soul, Stoicism is wanting. It does not understand either the love of God or the love of man. It does not understand love's passion or its purity. In spite of its emphasis upon the social nature of man, it does not understand the true interrelationship of human souls with each other, in sorrow and in joy, for grief and for comfort. It posits a false independence. It does not perceive how the soul cannot realise itself without rejoicing in another's goodness and happiness, without grieving over another's sorrow and sin. But in spite of all its limitations, it has emphasized a true aspect of man's nature and of his greatness: it has emphasized the essential, even if it has run down the accidental too violently. " The aids to noble life are all within." " Know that he who finds himself, loses his misery." " It matters not how strait the gate, how charged with punishments the scroll, I am the master of my fate, I am the captain of my soul."[165]

One more point of high agreement (as of difference) let us notice. Into a rational world, a world of law and of order, into a Kosmos of majesty and beauty, we are born. We come into a commonwealth, a kingdom. To obey *its* laws (which are *our*

laws) is freedom. In Seneca's fine words: " In regno nati sumus;
deo parere libertas est."[166] In both terms is consolation. There
is comfort in the obedience; there is comfort in the liberty. Both
words are known to the Jew as well as to the Stoic. " There is
no freedom except in the Torah." Yet, perhaps, the Jew accentuates the side of obedience. " Deo parere." Obedience to
perfection: to perfect wisdom; perfect righteousness; perfect love. The happiness of obedience, the reverence and
adoration of it: on these he dwells. Perhaps the Stoic accentuates the side of freedom: the conquest of pleasure and pain: the
overthrow of the external. The soul in its strength and righteousness, and the soul in its wisdom and beauty; the soul in its
independence and aloneness. And yet even to the Stoic, the soul
was not alone, and its greatness and its glory were due to its
kinship with the universal reason which is God. To the Stoic,
as to the Jew, the ultimate comfort was in something beyond.
Even the soul is not enough—though between it and the Eternal
all else, in the last resort, must fade away. " Whom have I in
heaven but Thee, and there is none upon earth that I desire
beside Thee."

Yet though it is a horrid thing to pick holes in any great
spiritual message, it would be improper, and in a higher sense,
unfair, not to add a final word. The comfort of Judaism goes
deeper, and reaches further, than the comfort of Stoicism. The
Stoic message lacks simplicity and warmth. The appeal is, of
necessity, less to the many than to the few. It scarcely attempts
to meet the case of simple souls who may be able to love a Divine
Father, but whom a Universal Reason, or the Ruling Principle of
the world, will leave cold and unmoved. I would not,
perhaps, go quite so far as Matthew Arnold, who says
that " it is impossible to rise from reading Epictetus or
Marcus Aurelius without a sense of constraint and melancholy,
without feeling that the burden laid upon man is well
nigh greater than he can bear." But it is true that
they ask from us a certain intellectual effort, a certain brac-
ing of the mind, before their message can be appreciated or even
understood. And there are many who cannot, or will not, give
that effort; and for whom Epictetus and Aurelius, who, moreover, speak the language of a vanished age, and give their
message through unfamiliar terms, must always be a dead letter
and a sealed book. Judaism speaks to all: to the simple as well
as to the learned, to the foolish as well as to the wise.

Where the Stoic speaks of Reason, the Jew speaks of Goodness, and where the one adores the Divine Intelligence, the other worships the Divine Love. The contrast is not fixed or hard, but it is sufficiently true to be significant and not unfair. The God of the Psalter and of the Prophets may be, for some of us, too " personal," too " external "; but just for that very reason is He so near, so loving, so approachable. To comfort us to-day, the God in whom we believe must *want* to help us, must *want* to redeem, to save. And not only to save the wise, but still more those whom we feel ourselves to be—the erring, the weak, the foolish, the lame ducks, whom the Stoic God, in His serenity, will leave unaided and unhealed. The loving God yearns over His children : " Comfort ye, comfort ye," He bids His messenger : He does more than make even the recalcitrant submit to His supreme and everlasting will. We need warmth and tenderness : these comfort and assuage. " He healeth the broken-hearted and bindeth up their wounds. The Lord is my shepherd : I shall not want." If this be true, it is the deepest consolation. Seneca's God may test men as a father. The God of Judaism does more. " As one whom his *mother* comforts, so will I comfort you." " He will wipe away tears from off *all* faces." " He will seek that which is lost, He will bring again that which is driven away, He will bind up that which is broken, He will strengthen that which is sick."

The truth is that we need dependence as well as independence. The greatness of man and of his mind it is well to remember : to resist the shocks of fortune with fearless self sufficiency is good. Yet are these things not adequate. We need (and reason by no means gives to that need the lie) a Power immensely greater and nobler than our own. We need an infinite wisdom, an infinite righteousness, before whom we can bow down in humblest adoration, and in whom we can *rest*. Rest in the Lord; that is a wonderful comfort, for those who can feel it and believe it. " He is my banner and my refuge; He is my fortress and my strength. For underneath are the everlasting arms : the Lord is with me, and I will not fear." In the hour of bitterest sorrow the *Adon Olam* can be a greater consolation than the whole literature of Stoicism.

Perhaps, too, we need some more definite relation of God to the world and to humanity than Stoicism supplies. Noble indeed and valuable, very requisite and tonic for Jewish readers, is the grand Stoic cosmopolitanism. Its greatness and its truth abide for ever. But we painfully miss the idea of progress. We miss its comfort, its fortification. In addition to the real ideality of cosmopolitanism, we want also the real ideality of patriotism; the call and function of different countries and races in the outward movement of mankind. The election of Israel can be a great comfort to us: perhaps, too, for many of us, the election of England. The universe is too vast for us, we want a narrower purpose and a more restricted goal for our endeavour. Such purpose and goal can never supply the place of the "life to come." To many and many a problem they give no answer. But still we want them. Even if our earth is to end in sudden conflagration, or primaeval ice is to return, we want them still; be they consistent or no with such terminations, our heart cries out for them, as beacon lights for our action, as comforts for our sorrow. It is this imperishable hope which is afforded us by the visions of the Golden Age. "The earth shall be full of the knowledge of the Lord as the waters cover the sea. And in that day the Lord shall be One and His name One. And men shall beat their swords into plough-shares and their spears into pruning hooks; nation shall not lift up sword against nation, neither shall they learn war any more."

NOTES.

1. Herodotus, v. 4.
2. Ecclesiasticus, xli. 1, 2.
3. As to the true translation and meaning of the second Word, see Driver's note in his edition of Exodus in the Cambridge Bible for Schools and Colleges (1911). As he says, Deut. vii., 9, is a rhetorical amplification, not an exact interpretation. There is an interesting Talmudic discussion of the matter in Berachoth, 7a. Perhaps there may be several persons who may like a literal translation. R. Jose said, " Moses said to God, why is there a righteous man who prospers and a righteous man who suffers : why is there a wicked man who prospers and a wicked man who suffers? God replied, The righteous man who prospers is righteous and the son of a righteous man ; the righteous man who fares ill is righteous and the son of a wicked man ; the prosperous wicked is the son of a righteous man ; the wicked man who fares ill is the son of a wicked man." But the Talmud asks how can this be? Exodus xx., 5, and Deut. xxiv., 16, are contrasted, and it is said, Exodus xx., 5, only applies if the children continue in the evil ways of their parents, whereas Deut. xxiv., 16, applies (for God as well as man) if they do not so continue. " So to the question God rather replied thus : The righteous who prospers is completely righteous ; the righteous who fares ill is not completely righteous ; the wicked who prospers is not completely wicked ; the wicked who suffers is completely wicked." But R. Meir did not agree with this teaching. Exodus xxxiii., 19, 20, implied, according to him, that God gives prosperity to those who do not merit it." Cp. Schechter, The Doctrine of Divine Retribution in Rabbinical Literature in Studies in Judaism (first series), pp. 259—282. A passage in the Mechilta (68b, ed. Friedmann, Wuensche, p. 213) is also worth quoting. " He visits the iniquity of the fathers upon the children. That is, if they do not break the chain. But He does not so visit if they do. He visits the iniquity of the wicked grandfather upon the wicked grandson if the wicked grandson has a wicked father : but if the wicked father has a good son, the " visiting " is broken. When Moses heard that, he said, God forbid that there should be in Israel a wicked man whose father and grandfather were both wicked. Again, it might be thought that as the measure of punishment continues for four generations, so the measure of reward only continues for four generations. Therefore it says, showing mercy unto thousands. And lest one should suppose, only two thousands, it says (Deut. vii., 9), to the thousandth generation, that is, without number or limit." (Cp. Pesikta Kahana, 167a ad fin 167b init. Wuensche, p. 242.
4. I. Sam., iii., 18.
5. Jeremiah, xii., 1.
6. II. Sam., x., 12.
7. Amos, iii., 6.
8. Job, xiv., 1, 2 ; vii., 1 ; xxi., 19-21, 23-26.
9. Jer., xvii., 9 ; II. Sam., xxiv., 1 ; I. Ch., xxi., 1 ; Lev., xxvi., 39 ; Ezekiel, iv., 17 ; xxiv., 23 ; xxxiii., 10 ; Isaiah, lxiii., 17.

10. Wellhausen, Israelitische und Jueditische Geschichte, p. 213 (ed. 6, 1907). The fifteenth chapter is perhaps too condensed to be wholly accurate, but it is a brilliant masterpiece for all that.

11. Isaiah, xxvi., 8, and Dr. Skinner's note in his edition of Isaiah in the Cambridge Bible for Schools and Colleges.

12. Psalm, cxix., 71; Proverbs, iii., 11, 12. The translation given depends upon a probable and slight emendation of the Hebrew text. It was the reading of the Septuagint.

13. Psalm xciv., 12; Job, v., 17, xxxvi., 15.

14. Zech., xiii., 9. Isaiah, xlviii., 10, with the notes of Marti and Box. Psalm, lxvi., 10-12.

15. Psalm xliv., 22. I. Macc., ix., 10.

16. Psalm cxlvii., 3; xciv., 19; lxxiii., 25, 26; cxix., 50, 92, 143.

17. Ezekiel, xviii., 30, 31; xxxvi., 26; xi., 19.

18. Daniel, xii., 2; cp. Isaiah, xxvi., 19.

19. Kiddushin, 40b. Leviticus R., xxvii., init. Wuensche, p. 183.

20. Rosh ha' Shanah, 17a.

21. Wisdom of Solomon, iv., 1-5.

22. II. Macc., vii., 9, 14, 29.

23. Aboth, iv., 23 (ed. Taylor).

24. Sabbath, 55b.

25. Authorized Prayer Book, ed. Singer, p. 121.

26. Sanhedrin, 101a. Note also the subsequent story in which Akiba brings in his favourite saying, " Beloved are chastisements."

27. Genesis R., xcii., init. Wuensche, p. 452. Note the other sayings in the same section.

28. Sanhedrin, 101, a. fin; 101b, init.

29. Genesis R., lxv. Wuensche, p. 310. Arachin, 16b.

30. Menachoth, 53b.

31. Chullin, 7b.

32. Genesis R., xcii., ad init. Wuensche, p. 453.

33. Genesis R., lxv. Wuensche, p. 310.

34. Mechilta on Exodus xx., 23; Wuensche, p. 227, 228. Sifri, 73b. on Deut. vi., 5. (ed. Friedmann.)

35. I infer this from Berachoth, 5a. See infra.

36. Genesis R., ix., fin. Wuensche, p. 39.

37. Genesis R., xxxii. Wuensche, p. 138. Genesis R., xxxiv., init. Wuensche, p. 149. Canticles R., on ii., 16. Wuensche, p. 80.

38. Berachoth, 5a.

39. Semachoth, Ch. iii. Cp. Sabbath, 118b.

40. Ecclesiastes R., on vii., 27. Wuensche, p. 110.

41. Mechilta on Exodus xx., 23. Wuensche, p. 227; do. on xix., 9. Wuensche, p. 198.

42. Mishnah Berachoth, ix., 54a.

43. Berachoth, 62a.

44. Taanith, 8a.

45. Midrash Tillim, on xxvi., 1. Wuensche, Vol. i., p. 229, 230.

46. Authorized Prayerbook, ed Singer, p. 292. Mishnah Berachoth ix., 54a.

47. Berachoth, 60b.

48. Midrash Samuel, xix. Wuensche, p. 106. Bacher, Agada der

ii.

palaestinensischen Amoraeer, Vol. iii., p. 121. Midrash Tillim, xvi., 3. Wuensche, Vol. I., p. 124.

49. Mechilta on Exodus, xx., 5. Wuensche, p. 213.

50. Pesikta K., x., 87a. Wuensche, p. 112.

51. Midrash Tillim, ix., fin. Wuensche, Vol. I., p. 93.

52. Midrash Tillim, xvi., 3. Wuensche, Vol. I., p. 124.

52a. Exodus R., xxxv. Wuensche, p. 266.

53. Berachoth, 61b. Jer Berachoth, ix., Schwab, Vol. I., p. 169, 170.

54. Sabbath, 33b.

55. Sanhedrin, 39a.

55a. That Moses is said to have broken the Tables that he might either die with Israel or be forgiven with them hardly invalidates my statement. Exodus R., xlvi. Wuensche, p. 319.

56. Yalkut Proverbs, § 564. Midrash Proverbs on xxxi, 10. Wuensche, p. 71, 72.

57. Aboth R. Natan, xiv., 30a. Ed. Schechter. Pollak, p. 69.

58. Aboth, iv., 21. (Ed. Taylor).

58a. Sabbath, 55a, Menachoth, 29b. Schechter. Studies in Judaism, p. 276.

59. Porter : The Yetzer ha Ra, p. 117, in Biblical and Semitic Studies by the members of the Semitic and Biblical Faculty of Yale University (London, Arnold, 1901).

60. Baba Batra, 16a. Kiddushin, 30b. Yoma, 69b, and many other passages. Porter, p. 126, 127.

61. Genesis R., ix. Wuensche, p. 38. Porter, p. 114.

62. Porter, p. 125. Aboth R. Natan, xvi., 32b. Pollak, p. 76. Midrash Tillim on Psalm lxxxvi., 11. Wuensche, Vol. II., p. 46 fin.

63. Berachoth, ix., 54a.

64. Porter, p. 118. Canticles R., on i., 2. Wuensche, p. 15.

64a. Taanith, 25a. Schechter, Studies, p. 278.

64b. The place of Immortality in religious belief, by Dr. Estlin Carpenter (1898), p. 93.

64c. Berachoth, 58b. Schechter, Studies, p. 279.

65. Sabbath, 88b.

66. Ecclesiastes R. on vii., 1. Wuensche, p. 89.

67. Cp. Butcher's essay on " The Melancholy of the Greeks " in Some Aspects of the Greek Genius, p. 148.

68. Quoted in Livingstone's The Greek Genius and Its Meaning to Us (Ed. 2), p. 93.

69. Thucydides, ii., 64 ad. fin. (Jowett's translation).

70. Theognis, 441-446.

71. Pythian Odes, iii., 93. iii., 80-83.

72. Herodotus, vii., 47 and 50.

73. Seneca. Consolation to Polybius, xvii.

74. Hippolytus. E. P. Coleridge's translation, 190-197 ; 203-207.

75. Illiad, xii., 322-328. Lang's translation.

76. De Corona, §97.

77. Nemean Odes, xi., 55-60.

78. Cp. Livingstone. Greek Genius, p. 133.

79. Job, v., 26.

80. Herodotus i., 32. Aristotle's Ethics, i., 10.

81. Mr. Mackail's translation in his Select Epigrams from the Greek Anthology, Ed. 2, p. 149.

iii.

82. Thucydides, ii., 44; 41. Jowett's translation.
83. Cyropaedia, vii., 3, 11.
84. Herodotus, i., 31.
85. Herodotus, i., 207.
86. Agamemnon, 188-193. Headlam's translation.
87. Sophocles, Fragments, 581.
88. Gorgias, 472; Laws, 728; Gorgias, 479; Republic, 613.
90. Phaedo, 114, fin.
91. Aristotle's Ethics, i., Chapters 9 and 10.
92. Ethics, x., 7. Milton, Paradise Lost, ii., 146-148. Goethe Faust, Part II., Act I., 73.
93. Plutarch On Contentedness of Mind, xx. Aesopus in Bergk's Poetae Lyrici Graeci, Vol. II., 64; Eudemean Ethics, 1216a. I owe the reference to Aesopus to Burckhardt, Griechische Kulturgeschichte, Vol. II., p. 388 (Ed. 2.) The section, Zur Gesamtbilanz des grieschishen Lebens contains a very bitter and one-sided estimate of Greek morality, but is well worth reading.
94. Plutarch's consolatory essays to his wife and to Apollonius.
95. Epictetus, iii., 24.. Matheson, p. 101.
96. ib., ii., 16, p. 194, 195, 196 init.
97. ib., i., 29, p. 132.
98. ib., iii., 17, p. 51.
99. Aurelius, iv., 8.
100. ib., iv., 7.
101. ib., vii., 14.
102. ib., ix., 13.
103. ib., viii., 48.
104. ib., iv., 49.
105. Epictetus. Encheiridion, or Manual, xi., p. 217.
106. ib., xvi., p. 219.
107. Discourses, iii., 24, p. 97.
108. ib., iii., 24, p. 93.
109. ib., iii., 24, p. 87.
110. ib., iv., 1, p. 130.
111. ib., iii., 26, p. 108.
112. ib., iii., 24, p. 92. Seneca. On a happy life, ix. On benefits, iv., 12.
113. Epictetus, Discourses, iii., 18, p. 52; iv., 1, p. 131.
114. ib., i., 18, p. 100. Manual xvi., p. 219. For a criticism on this doctrine, cp. Bevan, Stoics and Sceptics, p. 66-70, and Gilbert Murray's brilliant lecture: The Stoic Philosophy, p. 45-47.
115. i., 29, p. 137.
116. ib., iii., 5, p. 20.
117. ib., ii., 16, p. 200.
118. ib., ii., 16, fin., p. 200.
119. ib., iv., 1, p. 127.
120. ib., iv., 1, p. 128.
121. ib., iii., 13, p. 43.
122. Aurelius, ii., 11; viii., 46.
123. x., 28.
124. iv., 23.

125. ix., 40.

126. xii., 32.

127. Epictetus, Discourses, iii., 24, fin., p. 101; Seneca, of Providence, i., 6.

128. Discourses, iii., 20, p. 55.

129. iii., 10, p. 35.

130. iii., 10, p. 36.

131. Seneca, Of Providence, i., 1, 2 and 4.

132. For the hymn of Cleanthes cp. Davidson : The Stoic Creed, p. 235, and Adam : The Vitality of Platonism, p. 104-189. For the second fragment see Epictetus, Manual, liii., p. 238. For Seneca's Latin translation see his Epistles, 107.

133. Aurelius, vi., 42.

134. vi., 42.

135. ix., 28.

136. vi., 36.

137. vi., 10.

138. ix., 42 ; v., 17.

139. viii., 56.

140. ix., 11 ; vii., 22. The "philanthropy of the Stoics," coupled with the doctrine of ignorance and of involuntary vice, led them on to a great gentleness and a universal charity. The famous Stoic Thrasea, one of Nero's noblest victims, with the description of whose death Tacitus's Annals break off, went so far as to say that, " He who hates vice, hates mankind." The passage in Pliny's letters, in which these words occur, is worth quoting : " To my mind the best and most faultless character is his, who is as ready to pardon the rest of mankind, as though he daily transgressed himself ; and, at the same time, as cautious to avoid a fault, as if he never forgave anybody. Be it our rule, then, at home, abroad, and in every sphere of conduct, to be relentless to ourselves, placable to others, even to such as forgive no one but themselves ; remembering always what that most gentle, and for that reason (as well as for others) that very great man, Thrasea, used frequently to say : He who hates vices, hates mankind." (Pliny : Letters, viii., 22.)

141. Epictetus, Manual, xx., p. 220.

142. Discourses, i., 17, p. 97.

143. i., 28, p. 128.

144. i., 18, p. 98, 99.

145. iii., 22, p. 68.

146. Aurelius, vi., 7.

147. vi., 44.

148. Epictetus, Discourses, i., 14, p. 88, 90.

149. ii., 14, p. 188.

150. i., 9, p. 71.

151. i., 3, p. 52.

152. Aurelius, v., 33.

153. vi., 47.

154. vi., 30.

155. ii., 17 ; iv., 33.

156. xii., 29.

157. Epictetus, Discourses, ii., 1, p. 144.

158. ii., 6, p. 160; iii., 24, p. 98.

158a. It is needless to give the references to suicide in Epictetus and Aurelius. The subject indexes to the translations supply them for those who care to look. But as illustrating the great difference between the Stoic and the Jewish view, the story of the martyrdom of R. Chanina ben Teradion may be of interest. The story is told in two divisions, and clearly is partly legendary and partly historical. I shall have to make some omissions. " When R. Eleazar b. Proto and R. Chanina b. Teradion were arrested, Eleazar said to Chanina, Happy are you, that you have been arrested on one count, whereas I have been arrested on five. Chanina answered, Happy are you, who will be set free; woe is me, who will not be delivered. You occupied yourself with the study of the Law, and with deeds of charity, whereas I only occupied myself with the study of the Law. Chanina said this according to the teaching of R. Huna, who declared, He who only occupies himself with the study of the Law is as if he had no God." I here make a long omission. " They brought out R. Chanina and asked him, Why did you occupy yourself with the study of the Law? He answered, Because God commanded me to do so. They then sentenced him to be burnt alive, his wife to be decapitated, and his daughter to be put in a brothel." Then the Talmud, as happens so frequently, falls a victim to its inveterate desire to find a reason in human sin for human suffering; sinking, as it sinks so often, to the irreligious level of Job's friends, and forgetting the highest teaching both of the Old Testament and of itself. I omit the silly reasons which are given for all three sufferers. The story is then resumed with a fresh introduction. " When R. Jose b. Kisura was ill, R. Chanina b. Teradion went to visit him. Jose said to him, Brother, do you not know that God has given dominion to this nation (i.e., Rome); that it has destroyed His house, burnt His sanctuary, slaughtered His saints, and that it still is established? And I hear that you still occupy yourself with the study of the Law and carry a scroll of the Law in your bosom. Chanina said, Heaven will have mercy upon me. Jose replied, I say sensible words to you, and you answer, heaven will have mercy upon me! I shall be surprised if they do not burn you and your scroll with fire. Then Chanina said, What will be my lot as regards the life of the world to come? Jose said, Have you anything to show?" Once more we note the old doctrine in another form. What good deed have you done to merit the guerdon of the blessedness of the life to come? " Chanina said, Purim money got mixed up with alms money, and I gave it all to the poor." This apparently means that he supplied and put back the Purim distribution money from his own pocket. " Then Jose said, In that case may my portion be like unto your portion, and may my lot be as yours. After a few days R. Jose died and all the great ones of Rome (the Roman authorities in Palestine) attended his funeral, and they mourned for him with a great mourning. When they returned, they met Chanina occupying himself with the study of the Law, holding assemblies in public, and carrying a scroll in his bosom. Then they took him, and wrapped the scroll round him, heaped bundles of willow wood about him, and set fire to them. Then they took woolly bits of cloth, soaked them in water, and laid them on his heart that he might not die quickly. Then his daughter said, Father, that I should have to see you thus ! He replied, If I were to be burnt alone, it would have been hard for me, but now that the Scroll of the Law is being burnt with me, He who will avenge His own humiliation in the burning of the Scroll will also avenge my humiliation. His disciples said to him, What do you see? He replied, The leaves of the Scroll are being burnt and the letters are flying (up to heaven)." The idea is that the divine word has an indestructible existence of its own, independent of the material to which it is temporally attached. " Then they said to him, Open your mouth that the fire may enter into it." (The object was that his tortures should be shortened). " He replied, It is better that He who gave me my soul should take it rather than that (I should break the rule) let no man do himself an injury (or let no man do violence to himself.)" Here the marked difference between Judaism and Stoicism becomes apparent. " Then the executioner said to him, Master, if I increase the flame, and remove the bits of woolly cloth from your heart, will you bring me into the life of the world to come? Chanina replied, Yes, I will. He said, Swear it to me. Then Chanina swore it. At once the executioner increased the flame, and removed the bits of woolly cloth from his heart, and his soul departed quickly. Then the executioner himself leaped into the fire (and was burnt). Then a heavenly voice was heard to say, R. Chanina b. Teradion and the Executioner are appointed for the life of the world to come. And Rabbi wept and said, Some attain their World (to come) in an hour, and some win it (only) in many years." The Talmud goes on to tell of the strange rescue of Chanina's daughter, pure and unharmed, from the brothel by her brother-in-law, R. Meir. (Aboda Zara, 17b.-18b. cp. Bacher, Agada der Tannaiten, Vol. I., p. 394-398, Ed. 2). Another curious story is that of the martyrdom of R. Ishmael and R. Simeon. The latter says to the former : " I am grieved, for I know not why I am to be killed. Then R. Ishmael said, Did you ever when a man brought a suit before you, or asked you for a decision, put him off till you had drunk, or put on your shoes, or wrapped yourself in your mantle? For the ' oppression ' which the Law forbids (Exodus, xxii., 23) may be great or small. R. Simeon said, Thou hast comforted me, my teacher." On the other hand, Akiba regarded the martyrdom of these two great men as an indication that sore evil was at hand, ·and he quoted Isaiah lvii., 1, 2 (Mechilta, p. 956, Wuensche, p. 306). The version of the story in Aboth R. Natan is different, but also interesting and touching. " Simeon was dazed, and said to Ishmael, Woe to us, we are to be killed like profaners of the Sabbath, or idolators, or incestuous persons, or murderers. Then Ishmael said, May I say something? He said, Speak. Ishmael said, Perhaps when you sat in your house, poor people came, and they stood outside, and you did not let them in, and give them food. Then Simeon said, I swear to heaven, I never did so. For I kept watchers before my house that they should at once bring in any poor who came to my door, and they ate and drank and blessed the name of God. Then Ishmael said, Perhaps when you sat upon the Temple Hill, and taught, and all the bands of the Israelites, were before you, your mind was puffed up. Then Simeon said, My brother, a man must be prepared to receive his fate." (I suppose he had pulled himself together) "Each besought the executioner to let him die first. One said, I am a priest, son of a high priest; let me die first, that I shall not see the death of my friend. The other said, I am a prince, the son of a prince, let me die first. The executioner said, Draw lots. The lot fell on Simeon, and the executioner cut off his head. Ishmael took it up, put it in his bosom, and wept and cried, Holy mouth, faithful mouth,

vii.

mouth that brought forth precious stones, who has rolled you in the dust, and filled your tongue with ashes? For you was it said, Awake, O Sword, against my friend. (Zech. xiii., 7.) He had not finished the words when his head fell." (Abot R. Natan, xxxviii., 57b., Pollak, p. 132). These stories are very revealing. The strength and piety of the Rabbinic religion shines out in them; to some extent too its limitations.

159. i., 9, p. 72.
160. Aurelius, ii., 5, 11; iv., 17.
161. ii., 3; xii., 21.
162. xii., 5.
163. ix., 3.
164. xii., 36.
165. Both the quotations from Matthew Arnold are used by Prof. Davidson in " the Stoic Creed." But Arnold's own position as a whole is very far from that of Epictetus or Aurelius. Henley's poem is even further away still in its ' saeva indignatio.' There is no question of ' punishments ' to the Stoic. Yet the last line of the famous stanza is nobly Stoic.

166. Of a happy life, xv, fin.

The quotations from Epictetus are almost all taken from the new translation by Mr. P. E. Matheson (Oxford University Press, 2 vols., 1917). Only in a few instances have I used the older translation of G. Long, with which so many of us have grown up and become familiar. The quotations from Marcus Aurelius are almost all taken from the new and delightful edition by Mr. Haines in the Loeb Library.

As the essay is not intended, or of any use, for scholars, I have always appended to the Midrashic quotations a reference to the available translation. Most of the Talmudic passages can be read in the useful, and I believe, very decently accurate, translation of Goldschmidt. The general reader (if he can read German, and—for the Jerusalem Talmud—if he can read French) need no longer be balked from obtaining a very fair, if second hand, knowledge of Rabbinic literature, if he chooses to take the trouble. If he knows a *little* Hebrew and a *little* Aramaic, he can check his crib, and improve his knowledge, by a reference to the original texts.